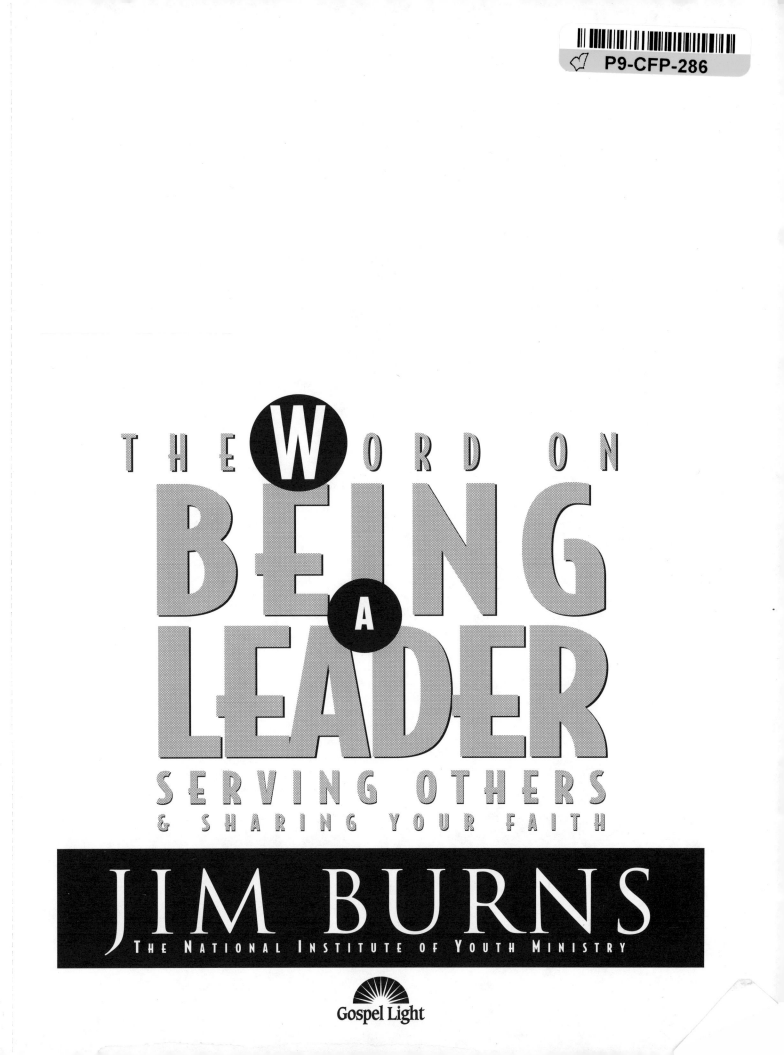

THE WORD ON BEING A LEADER

SERVING OTHERS
& SHARING YOUR FAITH

JIM BURNS
THE NATIONAL INSTITUTE OF YOUTH MINISTRY

Gospel Light

PUBLISHING STAFF

Jean Daly, Editor
Kyle Duncan, Editorial Director
Gary S. Greig, Ph.D., Editor in Chief
Joey O'Connor, Contributing Writer
Mario Ricketts, Designer

ISBN 0-8307-1645-9
© 1995 Jim Burns
All rights reserved.
Printed in U.S.A.

HOW TO MAKE CLEAN COPIES FROM THIS BOOK

Jim Burns knows young people. He also knows how to communicate to them. This study should be in the hands of every youth leader interested in discipling young people.

David Adams, Vice President, Lexington Baptist College

I deeply respect and appreciate the groundwork Jim Burns has prepared for true teenage discernment. YouthBuilders is timeless in the sense that the framework has made it possible to plug into any society, at any point in time, and to proceed to discuss, experience and arrive at sincere moral and Christian conclusions that will lead to growth and life changes. Reaching young people may be more difficult today than ever before, but God's grace is alive and well in Jim Burns and this wonderful curriculum.

Fr. Angelo J. Artemas, Youth Ministry Director, Greek Orthodox Archdiocese of North and South America

I heartily recommend Jim Burns's *YouthBuilders Group Bible Studies* because they are leader-friendly tools that are ready to use in youth groups and Sunday School classes. Jim addresses the tough questions that students are genuinely facing every day and, through his engaging style, challenges young people to make their own decisions to move from their current opinions to God's convictions taught in the Bible. Every youth group will benefit from this excellent curriculum.

Paul Borthwick, Minister of Missions, Grace Chapel

Jim Burns recognizes the fact that small groups are where life change happens. In this study he has captured the essence of that value. Further, Jim has given much thought to shaping this very effective material into a usable tool that serves the parent, leader and student.

Bo Boshers, Executive Director, Student Impact,
Willow Creek Community Church

It is about time that someone who knows kids, understands kids and works with kids writes youth curriculum that youth workers, both volunteer and professional, can use. Jim Burns's *YouthBuilders Group Bible Studies* is the curriculum that youth ministry has been waiting a long time for.

Ridge Burns, President,
The Center for Student Missions

There are very few people in the world who know how to communicate life-changing truth effectively to teens. Jim Burns is one of the best. *YouthBuilders Group Bible Studies* puts handles on those skills and makes them available to everyone. These studies are biblically sound, hands-on practical and just plain fun. This one gets a five-star endorsement—which isn't bad since there are only four stars to start with.

Ken Davis, President,
Dynamic Communications

I don't know anyone who knows and understands the needs of the youth worker like Jim Burns. His new curriculum not only reveals his knowledge of youth ministry but also his depth and sensitivity to the Scriptures. *YouthBuilders Group Bible Studies* is solid, easy to use and gets students out of their seats and into the Word. I've been waiting for something like this for a long time!

Doug Fields, Pastor of High School,
Saddleback Valley Community Church

Jim Burns has a way of being creative without being "hokey." *YouthBuilders Group Bible Studies* takes the age-old model of curriculum and gives it a new look with tools such as the Bible *Tuck-In*™ and Parent Page. Give this new resource a try and you'll see that Jim shoots straightforward on tough issues. The *YouthBuilders* series is great for leading small-group discussions as well as teaching a large class of junior high or high school students. The Parent Page will help you get support from your parents in that they will understand the topics you

are dealing with in your group. Put Jim's years of experience to work for you by equipping yourself with this quality material.

Curt Gibson, Pastor to Junior High,
First Church of the Nazarene of Pasadena

Once again, Jim Burns has managed to handle very timely issues with just the right touch. His *YouthBuilders Group Bible Studies* succeeds in teaching solid biblical values without being stuffy or preachy. The format is user-friendly, designed to stimulate high involvement and deep discussion. Especially impressive is the Parent Page, a long overdue tool to help parents become part of the Christian education loop. I look forward to using it with my kids!

David M. Hughes, Pastor,
First Baptist Church, Winston-Salem

What do you get when you combine a deep love for teens, over 20 years' experience in youth ministry and an excellent writer? You get Jim Burns's *YouthBuilders* series! This stuff has absolutely hit the nail on the head. Quality Sunday School and small-group material is tough to come by these days, but Jim has put every ounce of creativity he has into these books.

Greg Johnson, author of *Getting Ready for the Guy/Girl Thing* and *Keeping Your Cool While Sharing Your Faith*

Jim Burns has a gift, the gift of combining the relational and theological dynamics of our faith in a graceful, relevant and easy-to-chew-and-swallow way. *YouthBuilders Group Bible Studies* is a hit, not only for teens but for teachers.

Gregg Johnson, National Youth Director,
International Church of the Foursquare Gospel

The practicing youth worker always needs more ammunition. Here is a whole book full of practical, usable resources for those facing kids face-to-face. *YouthBuilders Group Bible Studies* will get that blank stare off the faces of kids in your youth meeting!
Jay Kesler, President, Taylor University

I couldn't be more excited about the *YouthBuilders Group Bible Studies*. It couldn't have arrived at a more needed time. Spiritually we approach the future engaged in war with young people taking direct hits from the devil. This series will practically help teens who feel partially equipped to "put on the whole armor of God."
Mike MacIntosh, Pastor,
Horizon Christian Fellowship

In *YouthBuilders Group Bible Studies*, Jim Burns pulls together the key ingredients for an effective curriculum series. Jim captures the combination of teen involvement and a solid biblical perspective, with topics that are relevant and straightforward. This series will be a valuable tool in the local church.
Dennis "Tiger" McLuen, Executive Director,
Youth Leadership

My ministry takes me to the lost kids in our nation's cities where youth games and activities are often irrelevant and plain Bible knowledge for the sake of learning is unattractive. Young people need the information necessary to make wise decisions related to everyday problems. *YouthBuilders* will help many young people integrate their faith into everyday life, which after all is our goal as youth workers.
Miles McPherson, President, Project Intercept

Jim Burns's passion for teens, youth workers and parents of teens is evident in the *YouthBuilders Group Bible Studies*. He has a gift of presenting biblical truths on a

level teens will fully understand, and youth workers and parents can easily communicate.
Al Menconi, President, Al Menconi Ministries

Youth ministry curriculum is often directed to only one spoke of the wheel of youth ministry—the adolescent. Not so with this material! Jim has enlarged the education circle, including information for the adolescent, the parent and the youth worker. *YouthBuilders Group Bible Studies* is youth and family ministry-oriented material at its best.
Helen Musick, Instructor of Youth Ministry,
Asbury Seminary

Finally, a Bible study that has it all! It's action-packed, practical and biblical; but that's only the beginning. *YouthBuilders* involves students in the Scriptures. It's relational, interactive and leads kids toward lifestyle changes. The unique aspect is a page for parents, something that's usually missing from adolescent curriculum. Jim Burns has outdone himself. This isn't a home run—it's a grand slam!
Dr. David Olshine, Director of Youth Ministries,
Columbia International University

Here is a thoughtful and relevant curriculum designed to meet the needs of youth workers, parents and students. It's creative, interactive and biblical—and with Jim Burns's name on it, you know you're getting a quality resource.
Laurie Polich, Youth Director,
First Presbyterian Church of Berkeley

In 10 years of youth ministry I've never used a curriculum because I've never found anything that actively involves students in the learning process, speaks to young people where they are and challenges them with biblical truth—I'll use this! *YouthBuilders Group Bible Studies* is a complete curriculum that is helpful to parents, youth leaders and, most importantly, today's youth.

Glenn Schroeder, Youth and Young Adult Ministries, Vineyard Christian Fellowship, Anaheim

This new material by Jim Burns represents a vitality in curriculum and, I believe, a more mature and faithful direction. *YouthBuilders Group Bible Studies* challenges youth by teaching them how to make decisions rather than telling them what decisions to make. Each session offers teaching concepts, presents options and asks for a decision. I believe it's healthy, the way Christ taught and represents the abilities, personhood and faithfulness of youth. I give it an A+!

J. David Stone, President, Stone & Associates

Jim Burns has done it again! This is a practical, timely and reality-based resource for equipping teens to live life in the fast-paced, pressure-packed adolescent world of the '90s. A very refreshing creative oasis in the curriculum desert!

Rich Van Pelt, President, Alongside Ministries

YouthBuilders Group Bible Studies is a tremendous new set of resources for reaching students. Jim has his finger on the pulse of youth today. He understands their mind-sets, and has prepared these studies in a way that will capture their attention and lead to greater maturity in Christ. I heartily recommend these studies.

Rick Warren, Senior Pastor, Saddleback Valley Community Church

CONTENTS

THANKS AND THANKS AGAIN!

This project is definitely a team effort. First of all, thank you to Cathy, Christy, Rebecca and Heidi Burns, the women of my life.

Thank you to Jill Corey, my incredible assistant and longtime friend.

Thank you to Doug Webster for your outstanding job as executive director of the National Institute of Youth Ministry (NIYM).

Thank you to the NIYM staff in San Clemente: Gary Lenhart, Roger Royster, Eric Lucy, Luchi Bierbower, Dean Bruns, Laurie Pilz, Russ Cline and Larry Acosta.

Thank you to our 150-plus associate trainers who have been my coworkers, friends and sacrificial guinea pigs.

Thank you to Kyle Duncan, Bill Greig III and Jean Daly for convincing me that Gospel Light is a great publisher that deeply believes in the mission to reach young people. I believe!

Thank you to the Youth Specialties world. Tic, Mike and Wayne, so many years ago, you brought on a wet-behind-the-ears youth worker with hair and taught me most everything I know about youth work today.

Thank you to the hundreds of donors, supporters and friends of NIYM. You are helping create an international grassroots movement that is helping young people make positive decisions that will affect them for the rest of their lives.

"Where there is no counsel, the people fall; But in the multitude of counselors there is safety"
(Proverbs 11:14, NKJV).
Jim Burns
San Clemente, CA

DEDICATION

To: Ron Jensen, M.D.

Thank you, Ron, for your influence on my life. Thank you for challenging me with your lifestyle. Thanks for sharing your journey and your life with so many of us "minister types." You are making a difference. I am blessed and honored by our growing friendship.

"Dear children, let us not love with words or tongue but with actions and in truth"
(1 John 3:18).

Thanks Ron.

YOUTHBUILDERS GROUP BIBLE STUDIES

It's Relational—Students learn best when they talk—not when you talk. There is always a get acquainted section in the Warm Up. All the experiences are based on building community in your group.

It's Biblical—With no apologies, this series in unashamedly Christian. Every session has a practical, relevant Bible study.

It's Experiential—Studies show that young people retain up to 85 percent of the material when they are *involved* in action-oriented, experiential learning. The sessions use role-plays, discussion starters, case studies, graphs and other experiential, educational methods. *We believe it's a sin to bore a young person with the gospel.*

It's Interactive—This study is geared to get students feeling comfortable with sharing ideas and interacting with peers and leaders.

It's Easy to Follow—The sessions have been prepared by Jim Burns to allow the leader to pick up the material and use it. There is little preparation time on your part. Jim did the work for you.

It's Adaptable—You can pick and choose from several topics or go straight through the material as a whole study.

It's Age Appropriate—In the "Team Effort" section, one group experience relates best to junior high students while the other works better with high school students. Look at both to determine which option is best for your group.

It's Parent Oriented—The Parent Page helps you to do youth ministry at its finest. Christian education should take place in the home as well as in the church. The Parent Page is your chance to come alongside the parents and help them have a good discussion with their kids.

It's Proven—This material was not written by someone in an ivory tower. It was written for young people and has already been used with them. They love it.

HOW TO USE THIS STUDY

The 12 sessions are divided into three stand-alone units. Each unit has four sessions. You may choose to teach all 12 sessions consecutively. Or you may use only one unit. Or you may present individual sessions. You know your group best so you choose.

Each of the 12 sessions is divided into five sections.

Warm Up—Young people will stay in your youth group if they feel comfortable and make friends in the group. This section is designed for you and the students to get to know each other better. These activities are filled with history-giving and affirming questions and experiences.

Team Effort—Following the model of Jesus, the Master Teacher, these activities engage young people in the session. Stories, group situations, surveys and more bring the session to the students. There is an option for junior high/middle school students and one for high school students.

In the Word—Most young people are biblically illiterate. These Bible studies present the Word of God and encourage students to see the relevance of the Scriptures to their lives.

Things to Think About—Young people need the opportunity to really think through the issues at hand. These discussion starters get students talking about the subject and interacting on important issues.

Parent Page—A youth worker can only do so much. Reproduce this page and get it into the hands of parents. This tool allows quality parent/teen communication that really brings the session home.

THE BIBLE *TUCK-IN*™

It's a tear-out sheet you fold and place in your Bible, containing the essentials you'll need for teaching your group.

HERE'S HOW TO USE IT:

To prepare for the session, first study the session. Tear out the Bible *Tuck-In*™ and personalize it by making notes. Fold the Bible *Tuck-In*™ in half on the dotted line. Slip it into your Bible for easy reference throughout the session. The Key Verse, Biblical Basis and Big Idea at the beginning of the Bible *Tuck-In*™ will help you keep the session on track. With the Bible *Tuck-In*™ your students will see that your teaching comes from the Bible and won't be distracted by a leader's guide.

Unit I

GIFTED TO SERVE

Leader's Pep Talk

Can I be perfectly honest? This may be the most important section of curriculum and teaching you have ever taught your students. Here's why I think so: our kids (and we) are living in a me-first, I-centered world. The "what's in it for me" lifestyle is so blatant these days. In the midst of all this mess, the call to Christ is the call to serve. In this section you are not just giving your students a nice and neat little lesson. You are challenging them toward a lifelong lifestyle of servanthood. They have been gifted by God with spiritual gifts to serve the Body of Christ, and there is nothing in my mind more exciting than helping kids use their giftedness for God.

If you are anything like me, you probably struggle at times with having a proper servant's heart. Here we are trying to teach our kids to serve while we struggle to live out servant leadership in our own lives.

I love and admire Chuck Swindoll's honesty in the statement:

> I'm like James and John. Lord, I size up other people in terms of what they can do for me, how they can further my program, feed my ego, satisfy my needs, give me strategic advantage. I exploit people ostensibly for your sake. Lord, I turn to you to get the inside track and obtain special favors. Your direction for my schemes, Your power for my projects, Your sanction for my ambitions, Your blank check approval for whatever I want. I'm a lot like James and John. And then the prayer, Change me, Lord. Make me a man or woman who asks of You and of others, "What can I do for you?"[1]

As you work through this session, that's my prayer for you. And that's my prayer for your kids.

Thanks for being a catalyst for change and service for the living, loving God.

Note

1. Charles R. Swindoll, *Improving Your Serve* (Waco, TX: Word Publishing, 1981), pp. 94-95.

CONGRATULATIONS, YOU'RE GIFTED

KEY VERSES

"Now about spiritual gifts, brothers, I do not want you to be ignorant. There are different kinds of gifts, but the same Spirit." 1 Corinthians 12:1,4

BIBLICAL BASIS

Matthew 25:14-30; Romans 12:6-8; 1 Corinthians 12:1,4-11,28-30; 13:1-3; Ephesians 4:7,8,11,12; Colossians 3:17; 1 Peter 4:9-11

THE BIG IDEA

God has given each person unique gifts, talents and abilities. Discovering and putting into practice the gifts God has given you will lead to a life of fulfillment and effective leadership.

AIMS OF THIS SESSION

During this session you will guide students to:
- Examine the basic principles of spiritual giftedness;
- Discover their spiritual gifts;
- Implement a plan to use their spiritual gifts in their church or youth group.

WARM UP

EVERYBODY HAS TALENT—

An inventory of the talent in the group.

TEAM EFFORT— JUNIOR HIGH/ MIDDLE SCHOOL

USING YOUR TALENTS AND GIFTEDNESS FOR GOD—

Students determine the responsibilities their group has and the talents they have to meet those responsibilities.

TEAM EFFORT— HIGH SCHOOL

IT'S YOUR WONDERFUL LIFE—

Students examine what life would be like without the talents of the others in their group.

IN THE WORD

WHAT'S MY GIFT?—

A Bible study on spiritual gifts.

THINGS TO THINK ABOUT (OPTIONAL)

Questions to get students thinking and talking about the significance of spiritual gifts.

PARENT PAGE

A tool to get the session into the home and allow parents and young people to discuss using their spiritual gifts to minister to others.

LEADER'S DEVOTIONAL

"If I speak in the tongues of men and of angels, but have not love, I am only a resounding gong or a clanging cymbal. If I have the gift of prophecy and can fathom all mysteries and all knowledge, and if I have a faith that can move mountains, but have not love, I am nothing. If I give all I possess to the poor and surrender my body to the flames, but have not love, I gain nothing" (1 Corinthians 13:1-3).

Young people aren't always very clear on what youth ministry is all about. Let me explain. On one of our high school water-ski trips, I was standing on top of the houseboat playing my guitar. Jeff, one of our student leaders, came up to me and said in a joking way, "I've finally figured out what it takes to be a good youth minister. All I have to know how to do is play the guitar and be a really good water- and snow-skier."

Since those were three of my favorite things to do, Jeff and I had a good laugh, but we both knew that being a good youth worker included a whole lot more than just knowing how to do things teenagers like to do. My friendship with Jeff wasn't based upon how well I played the guitar or how fast I could ski down a hill of steep moguls. All that other stuff was fun to do, but one of Jeff's real reasons for staying involved was because he knew I cared about him. Our friendship was based upon our mutual love for Jesus Christ.

If you want to know what really impresses teenagers, offering them the unconditional love of God is the best place to start. The greatest gift you can give to young people is the unconditional acceptance found in Jesus Christ. Teenagers today aren't concerned with how funny, talented, athletic, or good-looking you are. Teenagers want to know that you love and accept them for who they are. That's what really makes a difference in their lives!

Using your gifts and talents for God's glory is important, but don't miss the most important gift of all. Even if you are the most gifted, spiritual, talented, faith-filled youth minister that ever walked the face of planet earth, if you don't have love, the Bible says you are nothing and you gain nothing. Be God's instrument that loves kids into His kingdom. Offer them the greatest gift of all: The unconditional love of God found in Christ Jesus. (Written by Joey O'Connor.)

What you keep to yourself, you lose; what you give away, you keep forever.—Anonymous

CONGRATULATIONS, YOU'RE GIFTED

KEY VERSES

"Now about spiritual gifts, brothers, I do not want you to be ignorant. There are different kinds of gifts, but the same Spirit." 1 Corinthians 12:1,4

BIBLICAL BASIS

Matthew 25:14-30; Romans 12:6-8; 1 Corinthians 12:1,4-11,28-30; 13:1-3; Ephesians 4:7,8,11,12; Colossians 3:17; 1 Peter 4:9-11

THE BIG IDEA

God has given each person unique gifts, talents and abilities. Discovering and putting into practice the gifts God has given you will lead to a life of fulfillment and effective leadership.

WARM UP (5-10 MINUTES)
EVERYBODY HAS TALENT
- Divide students into pairs.
- Have students share three of their talents.
- As a whole group, share the talents. Then vote for the most unusual talent, the strangest talent, the nicest talent and the most valuable talent.

TEAM EFFORT—JUNIOR HIGH/ MIDDLE SCHOOL (15-20 MINUTES)
USING YOUR TALENTS AND GIFTEDNESS FOR GOD
- Give each student a copy of "Using Your Talents and Giftedness for God" on page 19 and a pen or pencil, or display a copy using an overhead projector.

– Fold –

• As a whole group, students complete their pages. The Scriptures say: **"Now about spiritual gifts, brothers, I do not want you to be ignorant. There are different kinds of gifts, but the same Spirit"** (1 Corinthians 12:1,4).

Jobs/Roles in Our Group/Church	Talent on Loan from God
....	....
....	....
....	....
....	....
....	....
....	....

ᴛ ᴇᴀᴍ ᴇꜰꜰᴏʀᴛ—ʜɪɢʜ ꜱᴄʜᴏᴏʟ

It's Your Wonderful Life

• Divide students into groups of three or four in which students know each other well.
• Have students describe what your youth group or church would be like if each member in their small group was not a part of your youth group or church. For example, what things wouldn't get accomplished, or what skills and talents would be lacking if this person was missing?
• As a whole group, discuss the responses.

ɪ ɴ ᴛʜᴇ ᴡᴏʀᴅ (25-30 Minutes)

What's My Gift?

• Divide students into groups of three or four.
• Assign each groups one of the following Scripture passages: Romans 12:6-8; 1 Corinthians 12:4-11,28-30; Ephesians 4:7-8,11,12; 1 Peter 4:9-11.
• Have students identify the spiritual gifts listed in their Scripture passages and, as a whole group, share findings.
• Give each student a copy of "What's My Gift?" on pages 21-25 and a pen or pencil, or display a copy using an overhead projector.
• Students complete their pages.

"There are different kinds of gifts, but the same Spirit. There are different kinds of service, but the same Lord. There are different kinds of working, but the same God works all of them in all men. Now to each one the manifestation of the Spirit is given for the common good" (1 Corinthians 12:4-7).

—————————————— Fold ——————————————

Read the list of 27 spiritual gifts developed by C. Peter Wagner in *Your Spiritual Gifts Can Help Your Church Grow.*

Now take an inventory of your spiritual giftedness. Write one of the following responses next to each of the 27 spiritual gifts listed:

Yes = I have this gift.
Maybe = It's quite possible I have this gift or will have it in the future.
Doubtful = I really don't think I have the gift, but I'm not sure.
Who, me? = Most likely I don't have this particular gift.
Huh? = I'm not even sure I know what the gift is, or what it's all about.

So What?

How can you use your spiritual gift(s) this week in your church or youth group?

....
....
....

ᴛ ʜɪɴɢꜱ ᴛᴏ ᴛʜɪɴᴋ ᴀʙᴏᴜᴛ (ᴏᴘᴛɪᴏɴᴀʟ)

• Use the questions on page 25 after or as a part of "In the Word."

1. Is the concept of God's having given you spiritual gifts a difficult concept to understand? Why or why not?

....
....

2. How can it be harmful to your faith to wish you had someone else's spiritual gifts?

....
....

3. How will your role as a gifted Christian challenge others to use their own gifts and abilities?

....
....

ᴘ ᴀʀᴇɴᴛ ᴘᴀɢᴇ

• Distribute page to parents.

TEAM EFFORT

USING YOUR TALENTS AND GIFTEDNESS FOR GOD

The Scriptures say: "Now about spiritual gifts, brothers, I do not want you to be ignorant. There are different kinds of gifts, but the same Spirit" (1 Corinthians 12:1,4).

List on a board all the jobs/roles in your youth group or church. Now list who in the group you think has the talents to do these jobs.

Jobs/Roles in Our Group/Church	Talent on Loan from God

IN THE WORD

WHAT'S MY GIFT?

"There are different kinds of gifts, but the same Spirit. There are different kinds of service, but the same Lord. There are different kinds of working, but the same God works all of them in all men. Now to each one the manifestation of the Spirit is given for the common good" (1 Corinthians 12:4-7).

Read the list of 27 spiritual gifts developed by C. Peter Wagner in *Your Spiritual Gifts Can Help Your Church Grow.*[1]

_____ 1. *Prophecy:* The gift of prophecy is the special ability that God gives to certain members of the Body of Christ to receive and communicate an immediate message of God to His people through a divinely anointed utterance.

_____ 2. *Service:* The gift of service is the special ability that God gives to certain members of the Body of Christ to identify the unmet needs involved in a task related to God's work, and to make use of available resources to meet those needs and help accomplish the desired goals.

_____ 3. *Teaching:* The gift of teaching is the special ability that God gives to certain members of the Body of Christ to communicate information relevant to the health and ministry of the Body and its members in such a way that others will learn.

_____ 4. *Exhortation:* The gift of exhortation is the special ability that God gives to certain members of the Body of Christ to minister words of comfort, consolation, encouragement and counsel to other members of the Body in such a way that they feel helped and healed.

_____ 5. *Giving:* The gift of giving is the special ability that God gives to certain members of the Body of Christ to contribute their material resources to the work of the Lord with liberality and cheerfulness.

_____ 6. *Leadership:* The gift of leadership is the special ability that God gives to certain members of the Body of Christ to set goals in accordance with God's purpose for the future and to communicate these goals to others in such a way that they voluntarily and harmoniously work together to accomplish those goals for the glory of God.

_____ 7. *Mercy:* The gift of mercy is the special ability that God gives to certain members of the Body of Christ to feel genuine empathy and compassion for individuals, both Christian and non-Christian, who suffer distressing physical, mental or emotional problems, and to translate that compassion into cheerfully done deeds that reflect Christ's love and alleviate the suffering.

_____ 8. *Wisdom:* The gift of wisdom is the special ability that God gives to certain members of the Body of Christ to know the mind of the Holy Spirit in such a way as to receive insight into how given knowledge may best be applied to specific needs arising in the Body of Christ.

_____ 9. *Knowledge:* The gift of knowledge is the special ability that God gives to certain members of the Body of Christ to discover, accumulate, analyze and clarify information and ideas that are pertinent to the growth and well-being of the Body.

_____ 10. *Faith:* The gift of faith is the special ability that God gives to certain members of the Body of Christ to discern with extraordinary confidence the will and purposes of God for the future of His work.

_____ 11. *Healing:* The gift of healing is the special ability that God gives to certain members of the Body of Christ to serve as human intermediaries through whom it pleases God to cure illness and restore health apart from the use of natural means.

_____ 12. *Miracles:* The gift of miracles is the special ability that God gives to certain members of the Body of Christ to serve as human intermediaries through whom it pleases God to perform powerful acts that are perceived by observers to have altered the ordinary course of nature.

_____ 13. *Discerning of spirits:* The gift of discerning of spirits is the special ability that God gives to certain members of the Body of Christ to know with assurance whether certain behavior purported to be of God is in reality divine, human or satanic.

_____ 14. *Tongues:* The gift of tongues is the special ability that God gives to certain members of the Body of Christ (A) to speak to God in a language they have never learned and/or (B) to receive and communicate an immediate message to God to His people through a divinely anointed utterance in a language they have never learned.

_____ 15. *Interpretation of tongues:* The gift of interpretation of tongues is the special ability that God gives to certain members of the Body of Christ to make known in the vernacular the message of one who speaks in tongues.

_____ 16. *Apostle:* The gift of apostle is the special ability that God gives to certain members of the Body of Christ to assume and exercise general leadership over a number of churches with an extraordinary authority in spiritual matters that is spontaneously recognized and appreciated by those churches.

_____ 17. *Helps:* The gift of helps is the special ability that God gives to certain members of the Body of Christ to invest the talents they have in the life and ministry of other members of the Body, thus enabling the person helped to increase the effectiveness of his or her spiritual gifts.

_____ 18. *Administration:* The gift of administration is the special ability that God gives to certain members of the Body of Christ to understand clearly the immediate and long-range goals of a particular unit of the Body of Christ and to devise and execute effective plans for the accomplishment of those goals.

_____ 19. *Evangelist:* The gift of evangelist is the special ability that God gives to certain members of the Body of Christ to share the gospel with unbelievers in such a way that men and women become Jesus' disciples and responsible members of the Body of Christ.

_____ 20. *Pastor:* The gift of pastor is the special ability that God gives to certain members of the Body of Christ to assume a long-term personal responsibility for the spiritual welfare of a group of believers.

_____ 21. *Celibacy:* The gift of celibacy is the special ability that God gives to certain members of the Body of Christ to remain single and enjoy it; to be unmarried and not suffer undue sexual temptations.

_____ 22. *Voluntary poverty:* The gift of voluntary poverty is the special ability that God gives to certain members of the Body of Christ to renounce material comfort and luxury and adopt a personal lifestyle equivalent to those living at the poverty level in a given society in order to serve God more effectively.

_____ 23. *Martyrdom:* The gift of martyrdom is the special ability that God gives to certain members of the Body of Christ to undergo suffering for the faith even to death while consistently displaying a joyous and victorious attitude that brings glory to God.

_____ 24. *Hospitality:* The gift of hospitality is the special ability that God gives to certain members of the Body of Christ to provide open house and warm welcome for those in need of food and lodging.

_____ 25. *Missionary:* The gift of missionary is the special ability that God gives to certain members of the Body of Christ to minister whatever other spiritual gifts they have in a second culture.

_____ 26. *Intercession:* The gift of intercession is the special ability that God gives to certain members of the Body of Christ to pray for extended periods of time on a regular basis and see frequent and specific answers to their prayers to a degree much greater than that which is expected of the average Christian.

_____ 27. *Deliverance (exorcism):* The gift of deliverance is the special ability that God gives to certain members of the Body of Christ to cast out demons and evil spirits.

Now take an inventory of your spiritual giftedness. Write one of the following responses next to each of the 27 spiritual gifts listed:

Yes = I have this gift.

Maybe = It's quite possible I have this gift or will have it in the future.

Doubtful = I really don't think I have the gift, but I'm not sure.

Who, me? = Most likely I don't have this particular gift.

Huh? = I'm not even sure I know what the gift is, or what it's all about.

So What?

How can you use your spiritual gift(s) this week in your church or youth group?

....

....

Note

1. C. Peter Wagner, *Your Spiritual Gifts Can Help Your Church Grow* (Ventura, CA: Regal Books, 1994), pp. 229-233. Used by permission.

THINGS TO THINK ABOUT

1. Is the concept of God giving you spiritual gifts a difficult concept to understand? Why or why not?

....

....

2. How can it be harmful to your faith to wish you had someone else's spiritual gifts?

....

....

3. How will your role as a gifted Christian challenge others to use their own gifts and abilities?

....

....

PARENT PAGE

1. Read Matthew 25:14-30. How does this story relate to using your God-given gifts for the kingdom of God?

....
....
....
....
....
....

2. Read Colossians 3:17. How does this verse relate to gifts, talents and abilities God has given you?

....
....
....
....
....
....

3. Discuss how as a family you can use your spiritual gifts to minister to each other.

....
....
....
....
....
....

Session 1 "Congratulations, You're Gifted"

Date ....

BECOMING OTHERS-CENTERED

 KEY VERSE

"Be devoted to one another in brotherly love. Honor one another above yourselves." Romans 12:10

 BIBLICAL BASIS

Matthew 25:37-40; Luke 9:24; Romans 12:10; Ephesians 4:12; 1 John 3:18

 THE BIG IDEA

The call to Christ is the call to serve.

AIMS OF THIS SESSION

During this session you will guide students to:
- Examine the biblical principles of becoming an others-centered person;
- Discover how they can develop the characteristics of servanthood and leadership;
- Implement a decision to become others-centered as a lifestyle.

 WARM UP

BECOMING OTHERS-CENTERED—

Students talk about people who serve others.

 TEAM EFFORT— JUNIOR HIGH/ MIDDLE SCHOOL

I CARE—

A list of students' concerns and actions of concern.

 TEAM EFFORT— HIGH SCHOOL

PRACTICING RANDOM ACTS OF KINDNESS AND SENSELESS DEEDS OF BEAUTY—

Students perform service projects.

 IN THE WORD

HOW TO BE AN OTHERS-CENTERED PERSON—

A Bible study on becoming an others-centered person.

 THINGS TO THINK ABOUT (OPTIONAL)

Questions to get students thinking and talking about serving others.

PARENT PAGE

A tool to get the session into the home and allow parents and young people to discuss how to serve each other and others.

LEADER'S DEVOTIONAL

"Then the righteous will answer him, 'Lord, when did we see you hungry and feed you, or thirsty and give you something to drink? When did we see you a stranger and invite you in, or needing clothes and clothe you? When did we see you sick or in prison and go to visit you?' The King will reply, 'I tell you the truth, whatever you did for one of the least of these brothers of mine, you did for me'" (Matthew 25:37-40).

One of the most inspiring teenagers I ever had in our youth ministry was a guy named Mike. When Mike was a junior and senior in high school, he was a linebacker on the best football team in the county. But being a football star wasn't the thing that impressed me about Mike. What really inspired me was Mike's authentic love and concern for others. Mike was a humble servant of Jesus Christ. Let me tell you about the story of Mike and Herb.

Herb was confined to a motorized wheelchair because of severe cerebral palsy. Herb wasn't a strong, popular football star like Mike. Herb drooled, his fingers were crumpled into little contorted fists and his words were barely intelligible. Herb wasn't the type of guy most other teenagers liked to hang around.

During our youth group pizza parties and hamburger nights, while other students were stuffing their faces, I would catch Mike out of the corner of my eye helping Herb with his dinner. Since Herb couldn't hold a hamburger, Mike would patiently serve Herb his dinner one bite at a time. When Herb needed a drink, Mike would hold a can of soda with a straw so Herb could take a sip. On more than a few occasions, I saw this incredible servant of God serving Herb as if he was serving Christ Himself. Mike transformed the message of the Scriptures into real-life practice. He was truly centered on serving Herb's needs and not his own.

Becoming others-centered begins with looking for Jesus in disguise. He may be in a Herb, a coworker or a student in the ministry you serve. As a youth worker, you have the tremendous opportunity to serve Jesus in all the students you know. Serving their needs will show them the authentic love of God in your life. Respond to the needs of young people is responding to the call of Christ. (Written by Joey O'Connor.)

"Unless life is lived for others, it is not worth-while."—Mother Teresa

SESSION TWO   BIBLE TUCK-IN ™

BECOMING OTHERS-CENTERED

KEY VERSE

"Be devoted to one another in brotherly love. Honor one another above yourselves."
Romans 12:10

BIBLICAL BASIS

Matthew 25:37-40; Luke 9:24; Romans 12:10; Ephesians 4:12; 1 John 3:18

THE BIG IDEA

The call to Christ is the call to serve.

WARM UP (5-10 MINUTES)

BECOMING OTHERS-CENTERED

• Divide students into groups of three or four.
• Display a copy of "Becoming Others-Centered" on page 33 using an overhead projector.
• Students discuss questions.

1. Who is the most others-centered person you know? What impresses you about him or her?

2. How have you been served by a person or group in the past six months? Have you experienced a significant act of kindness and service?

3. Share an experience you have had with serving someone.

--- Fold ---

31

---

3. Lose yourself in the service of others.

"For whoever would save his life will lose it, and whoever loses his life for me will save it" (Luke 9:24).

Try an experiment: Think of the happiest and most fulfilled person you know. The odds are this person you are thinking of is the most caring, unselfish, serving person you know also. You can lose your own problems as you serve and help others.

Complete this statement: I would be most helped to become a more others-centered person by...

4. You are the only Jesus somebody knows.

When you ask Jesus to come into your life, He promises to take up residence in your life. You become a representative of Jesus to others. Since many people never go to church, read the Bible or pray, the only way they may ever discover the forgiving and loving power of Jesus is by seeing Him in your life. That's why you are the only Jesus somebody knows!

Complete this statement: When I hear the phrase, "You are the only Jesus somebody knows" I feel...

   a. challenged.
   b. overwhelmed.
   c. scared.
   d. excited that He lives in me.
   e. I've got a long way to go.
   f. hopeful.

SO WHAT?

Complete these sentences and share them in a small group:
If there is one thing this Bible study on servanthood has taught me, it is...
I can be a more others-centered person by...

THINGS TO THINK ABOUT (OPTIONAL)

• Use the questions on page 41 after or as a part of "In the Word."

1. Jesus was called the "Suffering Servant" in the book of Isaiah. Why do you think He was called that?

2. Should we go on serving and caring for someone when there is little or no response from them?

3. What are specific ways we can develop a lifestyle of being others-centered?

PARENT PAGE

• Distribute page to parents.

TEAM EFFORT—JUNIOR HIGH/MIDDLE SCHOOL (15-20 MINUTES)

I CARE

- Ask the whole group what people their age care about.
- Divide students into pairs.
- Give each student a copy of "I Care" on page 35 and a pen or pencil.
- Students complete their pages.
- Optional: You could ask the group to find two or three "I care" issues that the youth group or their families could adopt as their "we care" projects.

List 10 things you care deeply about. If you are doing something specifically about what you care about, list that also.

I care:

1. ....
2. ....
3. ....
4. ....
5. ....
6. ....
7. ....
8. ....
9. ....
10. ....

What are some of the most creative "I care" issues?
....

What themes come up regularly?
....

As a whole group, create a list of areas of concerns.
Answer the following questions:
What do most students care about?
....

TEAM EFFORT—HIGH SCHOOL (15-20 MINUTES)

PRACTICING RANDOM ACTS OF KINDNESS AND SENSELESS DEEDS OF BEAUTY

- Divide students into groups of three or four.

Fold

- Within 12 minutes have each group perform a service project where they practice at least one random act of kindness or senseless deed of beauty. The purpose of this experience is to show the students that they can find a simple and creative way to serve in a short amount of time.
- Have each group share their experiences after everyone has completed their projects.

IN THE WORD (25-30 MINUTES)

HOW TO BE AN OTHERS-CENTERED PERSON

- Divide students into groups of three or four.
- Give each student a copy of "How to Be an Others-Centered Person" on pages 37-39 and a pen or pencil, or display a copy using an overhead projector.
- Students complete the Bible study.

Very often we think of the pastor on Sunday morning as the minister and the congregation as nonministers. That is just not true. We who call ourselves Christians are all ministers. The Greek word for minister also means to serve. It is the role and lifestyle of every Christian to be a servant—to be others-centered.

Our role and lifestyle in this world is to be a lover! In a world where people are hurting and suffering from lack of meaningful relationships, we are called to love them. Karl Menninger, a famous psychiatrist, says that 90 percent of all the people who come to him for help are seeking love. He says, "Love is the medicine of the world."

There are two types of people in the world—the I-centered, me-first people and the others-centered people. Which kind of a person are you? Place a mark on the continuum.

I-Centered   Others-Centered

Here's an interesting statement: "If...a person seeks not to receive love, but rather to give it, he or she will become lovable and will most certainly be loved in the end."

That statement is a paradox! We all want to be loved; however, instead of seeking to be loved, we need to go out and love, care and serve others. In doing this we become lovable, and we experience the joy of being loved by others. Read the statement again and put it into your own words.

Here are four points about being others-centered:
1. Actions speak louder than words!
"Dear children, let us not love with words or tongue but with actions and in truth" (1 John 3:18).
What actions could you do to be a lover?
What actions could you do to be a more others-centered person? (List at least five, being as specific as possible.)
2. Treat others as royalty.
"Love one another with brotherly affection; outdo one another in showing honor" (Romans 12:10, RSV).
What specifically can you do to treat others as royalty?

Name three people God is putting on your heart to treat in a special way. What do you plan to do to treat them as royalty?

Name	What You Plan to Do
a.	
b.	
c.	

WARM UP

BECOMING OTHERS-CENTERED

1. Who is the most others-centered person you know? What impresses you about him or her?

....

....

....

....

....

2. How have you been served by a person or group in the past six months? Have you experienced a significant act of kindness and service?

....

....

....

....

....

3. Share an experience you have had with serving someone or something that has been beneficial in your life.

....

....

....

....

....

TEAM EFFORT

I CARE

List 10 things you care deeply about. If you are doing something specifically about what you care about, list that also.
I Care...

1. ....
2. ....
3. ....
4. ....
5. ....
6. ....
7. ....
8. ....
9. ....
10. ....

As a whole group, create a list of areas of concerns.

Answer the following questions:

What do most students care about?

....
....
....

What themes come up regularly?

....
....
....

What are some of the most creative "I care" issues?

....
....
....
....

 N THE WORD

HOW TO BE AN OTHERS-CENTERED PERSON

Very often we think of the pastor on Sunday morning as the minister and the congregation as nonministers. That is just not true. We who call ourselves Christians are all ministers. The Greek word for minister also means to serve. It is the role and lifestyle of every Christian to be a servant—to be others-centered.

Our role and lifestyle in this world is to be a lover! In a world where people are hurting and suffering from lack of meaningful relationships, we are called to love them. Karl Menninger, a famous psychiatrist, says that 90 percent of all the people who come to him for help are seeking love. He says, "Love is the medicine of the world."

There are two types of people in the world—the I-centered, me-first people and the others-centered people. Which kind of a person are you? Place a mark on the continuum.

_____

I-Centered   **Others-Centered**

Here's an interesting statement: "If...a person seeks not to receive love, but rather to give it, he or she will become lovable and will most certainly be loved in the end."

That statement is a paradox! We all want to be loved; however, instead of seeking to be loved, we need to go out and love, care and serve others. In doing this we become lovable, and we experience the joy of being loved by others. Read the statement again and put it into your own words:

Here are four points about being others-centered:

1. Actions speak louder than words!

"Dear children, let us not love with words or tongue but with actions and in truth" (1 John 3:18).

What actions could you do to be a more others-centered person? (List at least five, being as specific as possible.)

....

....

2. Treat others as royalty

"Love one another with brotherly affection; outdo one another in showing honor" (Romans 12:10, *RSV*).

What specifically can you do to treat others as royalty?

....

....

Name three people God is putting on your heart to treat in a special way. What do you plan to do to treat them as royalty?

	Name	What You Plan to Do
a.	....	....
b.	....	....
c.	....	....

IN THE WORD

3. Lose yourself in the service of others.

"For whoever would save his life will lose it, and whoever loses his life for me will save it" (Luke 9:24).
Try an experiment: Think of the happiest and most fulfilled person you know. The odds are this person
you are thinking of is the most caring, unselfish, serving person you know also. You can lose your own
problems as you serve and help others.

Complete this statement: I would be most helped to become a more others-centered person by...

....

....

....

....

4. You are the only Jesus somebody knows.

When you ask Jesus to come into your life, He promises to take up residence in your life. You become a
representative of Jesus to others. Since many people never go to church, read the Bible or pray, the only
way they may ever discover the forgiving and loving power of Jesus is by seeing Him in your life. That's
why you are the only Jesus somebody knows!

Complete this statement: When I hear the phrase, "You are the only Jesus somebody knows" I feel...

   a. challenged.

   b. overwhelmed.

   c. scared.

   d. excited that He lives in me.

   e. I've got a long way to go.

   f. hopeful.

So What?

Complete these sentences and share them in a small group:

If there is one thing this Bible study on servanthood has taught me it is...

....

....

I can be a more others-centered person by...

....

....

....

 **T**HINGS TO **T**HINK **A**BOUT

1. Jesus was called the "Suffering Servant" in the book of Isaiah. Why do you think He was called that?

....

....

....

2. Should we go on serving and caring for someone when there is little or no response from them?

....

....

....

3. What are specific ways we can develop a lifestyle of being others-centered?

....

....

....

....

PARENT PAGE

THE CALL TO CHRIST IS THE CALL TO SERVE

The True or False Quiz

True	False	It is more blessed to give than to receive.
True	False	Happy people are more focused on others than themselves.
True	False	It's harder to be a servant to others as a teenager than as an adult.
True	False	In today's society it is almost impossible to be a servant.
True	False	Some people serve too much.
True	False	We are slaves for Christ.
True	False	Sometimes serving involves suffering.

"To prepare God's people for works of service, so that the body of Christ may be built up" (Ephesians 4:12).

How can we as a family serve each other?

....

What can our family do together to serve:

Our church?

....

Our neighborhood?

....

Our community?

....

Our world?

....

Here's an idea from Jim Burns: Sponsor a Compassion child.

I can't think of anything more important in life than helping make an impact on the world in which we live by sponsoring a child.

Our family has sponsored a child with Compassion for a number of years. That support of $24 a month—just 80 cents a day—covers the cost for clothing, health care and education for Ramiro Moises Santi. Our entire family looks forward to receiving Ramiro's letters, and we hope to visit him someday.

You, too, can sponsor a deserving boy or girl who needs love, protection and encouragement. As a sponsor, you'll receive your child's photo and personal story. Your child will know you by name and appreciate your love, help and prayer.

Start today by calling Compassion International's toll-free number, 1-800-336-7676.

Session 2 "Becoming Others-Centered"

Date ....

SERVING THE POOR AND OPPRESSED

KEY VERSE

"The King will reply, 'I tell you the truth, whatever you did for one of the least of these brothers of mine, you did for me.'" Matthew 25:40

BIBLICAL BASIS

Matthew 25:31-46; James 2:5

THE BIG IDEA

Every Christian is challenged by Jesus to serve the needs of those who are poor and oppressed.

AIMS OF THIS SESSION

During this session you will guide students to:
• Examine the words of Christ about helping the poor and oppressed;
• Discover practical ways to minister to the poor and oppressed;
• Implement new goals of ministry to the poor and oppressed.

WARM UP

MY WORLD—
A look at the life of a person from another world.

TEAM EFFORT— JUNIOR HIGH/ MIDDLE SCHOOL

"I FEEL" STATEMENTS—
Students examine how they feel about the needs of others.

TEAM EFFORT— HIGH SCHOOL

I WAS HUNGRY—
Students look at how some respond to the needs of others.

IN THE WORD

A SHEEP OR A GOAT—
A Bible study on serving Jesus by serving others.

THINGS TO THINK ABOUT (OPTIONAL)

Questions to get students thinking and talking about meeting the needs of others.

PARENT PAGE

A tool to get the session into the home and allow parents and young people to discuss ways to serve the needy.

LEADER'S DEVOTIONAL

"Listen, my dear brothers: Has not God chosen those who are poor in the eyes of the world to be rich in faith and to inherit the kingdom he promised those who love him?" (James 2:5).

Dynamic life transformations happen when young people learn to serve the poor and oppressed. Not too long ago, I was in Mexicali, Mexico, with our high school ministry for a week-long mission trip. One morning when I was meeting with some of our student leaders, a small barefoot Mexican boy stood nearby watching us. As we sipped our cups of warm hot chocolate on the cold morning, the boy nudged nearer and nearer to us. He finally walked right up and plopped down in the lap of a girl named Kerry. Seeing the discarded Styrofoam cups lying nearby, he began to pick up each one and sip out the remainder of the chocolate at the bottom of the cup. With a smile on his face, he drank from one cup to the next. This barefoot, dirty-faced little boy actually drank our leftovers! For all of us watching, we couldn't help but feel that God was teaching us an incredible lesson on poverty we wouldn't soon forget.

I'm convinced that youth ministries filled with fun and games all the time are perhaps not the most effective ministries. While there's nothing wrong with having fun and having crazy events, they can't compare to the life transformations that happen when students serve the poor and oppressed. As youth workers, we don't always have to fabricate the next BIG event. We don't need to entertain kids. We need to show them the poor who are loved by God. Telling teenagers about poverty won't change them. Television won't show them how they can make a difference. Direct, person-to-person, face-to-face contact with poor people just like the little Mexican boy with no shoes, is the most effective way for students to develop a heart for serving the least of God's children. Youth ministries that seek to serve the poor and oppressed are youth ministries of substance. Teaching young people to serve others is one of the best eternal investments you can make not only in their lives, but also in the lives of the people they serve. (Written by Joey O'Connor.)

"It is high time that the ideal of success should be replaced by the ideal of service."—Albert Einstein

Tear along perforation. Fold and place this Bible Tuck-In™ in your bible for session use.

SERVING THE POOR AND OPPRESSED

KEY VERSE

"The King will reply, 'I tell you the truth, whatever you did for one of the least of these brothers of mine, you did for me.'" Matthew 25:40

BIBLICAL BASIS

Matthew 25:31-46; James 2:5

THE BIG IDEA

Every Christian is challenged by Jesus to serve the needs of those who are poor and oppressed.

WARM UP (5-10 MINUTES)

MY WORLD

• Before class choose someone for a role-play. The person plays someone from a third-world country. Have him or her describe his or her life—work, food, home, income, etc. If possible, provide photographs. Then ask the group what they will do about what they just heard.

TEAM EFFORT—JUNIOR HIGH/ MIDDLE SCHOOL (15-20 MINUTES)

"I FEEL" STATEMENTS

• Give each student a copy of "'I Feel' Statements" on page 49 and a pen or pencil, or display a copy using an overhead projector.
• As a whole group, students complete their pages.
  • Forty-thousand people die of starvation each day on planet earth.
  • More than half of the people in the world have never heard about Jesus Christ.
  • Almost one-third of all young girls in America will be sexually abused by age 18.

---- Fold ----

3. Serving people means serving Jesus.

What point is Jesus making in verse 40?

Have you ever felt as though by helping another person you were in reality helping Jesus? If yes, when and how?

So What?

Circle the letter of the response that best describes you.
When it comes to the idea of serving people:
a. I have a long way to go.
b. I'm not sure what to do.
c. I'm beginning to head in the right direction.
d. I struggle with selfishness.
e. Other ....

What one principle from this study can you use as a new goal for your life today?

THINGS TO THINK ABOUT (OPTIONAL)

• Use the questions on page 55 after or as a part of "In the Word."
1. What makes it difficult to look at the world through the eyes of Jesus?

2. What should an individual Christian's response be to hunger and poverty?

3. What one thing could this group do to help fight both physical and spiritual hunger and poverty?

PARENT PAGE

• Distribute page to parents.

When I read these statements I feel...

"May my heart break with the things that break the heart of God." Bob Pierce, Founder of World Vision
What do you think Bob Pierce meant in this prayer?

What can you do personally and as a group to make a positive impact in this world?

TEAM EFFORT—HIGH SCHOOL (15-20 MINUTES)
I WAS HUNGRY
• Give each student a copy of "I Was Hungry" on page 51 and a pen or pencil, or display a copy using an overhead projector.
• As a whole group, students complete their pages.
"The King will reply, 'I tell you the truth, whatever you did for one of the least of these brothers of mine, you did for me'" (Matthew 25:40).

I Was Hungry
I was hungry
And you formed a humanities club
And discussed my hunger.
Thank you.
I was naked
And in your mind
You debated the morality of my
Appearance.
I was homeless
And you preached to me
Of the spiritual shelter of the
Love of God.
I was imprisoned
And you crept off quietly
To your chapel in the cellar
And prayed for my release.
I was sick
And you knelt and thanked God for
Your health.
I was lonely
And you left me alone
To pray for me.

Author Unknown

Fold

Have you seen the Christian Church sometimes act like this poem?

Read Matthew 25:40. What does Jesus say about serving the needy person?

IN THE WORD (25-30 MINUTES)
A SHEEP OR A GOAT
• Divide students into groups of three or four.
• Give each student a copy of "A Sheep or a Goat" on page 53 and a pen or pencil, or display a copy using an overhead projector.
• Students complete the Bible study.
Read Matthew 25:31-46.
We can learn at least three points from this parable:
1. God wants us to help in the simple things.
List the specific actions Jesus mentions in Matthew 25:31-46.

a.

b.

c.

Why would God want us to serve in the simple things?

What are other simple ways to help?

2. We should give simply for the sake of giving. True giving is with no strings attached.
What was the attitude of the people in verse 44? In verse 37?

What do you think it means to be generous?

TEAM EFFORT

"I FEEL" STATEMENTS

• Forty-thousand people die of starvation each day on planet earth.

• More than half of the people in the world have never heard about Jesus Christ.

• Almost one-third of all young girls in America will be sexually abused by age 18.

When I read these statements I feel...

....

....

....

"May my heart break with the things that break the heart of God." Bob Pierce, Founder of World Vision

What do you think Bob Pierce meant in this prayer?

....

....

....

....

What can you do personally and as a group to make a positive impact in this world?

....

....

....

....

....

TEAM EFFORT

I WAS HUNGRY

"The King will reply, 'I tell you the truth, whatever you did for one of the least of these brothers of mine, you did for me'" (Matthew 25:40).

I Was Hungry

I was hungry
And you formed a humanities club
And discussed my hunger.
Thank you.
I was naked
And in your mind
You debated the morality of my
Appearance.
I was homeless
And you preached to me
Of the spiritual shelter of the
Love of God.
I was imprisoned
And you crept off quietly
To your chapel in the cellar
And prayed for my release.
I was sick
And you knelt and thanked God for
Your health.
I was lonely
And you left me alone
To pray for me.

Author Unknown

Have you seen the Christian Church sometimes act like this poem?

....

....

....

Read Matthew 25:40. What does Jesus say about serving the needy person?

....

....

....

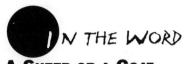

IN THE WORD

A SHEEP OR A GOAT

Read Matthew 25:31-46.

We can learn at least three points from this parable:

1. **God wants us to help in the simple things.**

   List the specific actions Jesus mentions in Matthew 25:31-46.

   ....

   ....

   What are other simple ways to help?

   a. ....

   b. ....

   c. ....

   Why would God want us to serve in the simple things?

   ....

2. **We should give simply for the sake of giving. True giving is with no strings attached.**

   What was the attitude of the people in verse 44? In verse 37?

   ....

   What do you think it means to be generous?

   ....

3. **Serving people means serving Jesus.**

   What point is Jesus making in verse 40?

   ....

   Have you ever felt as though by helping another person you were in reality helping Jesus? If yes, when and how?

   ....

   ....

SO WHAT?

Circle the letter of the response that best describes you.

When it comes to the idea of serving people:

   a. I have a long way to go.
   b. I'm not sure what to do.
   c. I'm beginning to head in the right direction.
   d. I struggle with selfishness.
   e. Other..

What one principle from this study can you use
as a new goal for your life today?

....

....

....

....

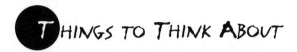

THINGS TO THINK ABOUT

1. What makes it difficult to look at the world through the eyes of Jesus?

....

....

....

2. What should an individual Christian's response be to hunger and poverty?

....

....

....

3. What one thing could this group do to help fight both physical and spiritual hunger and poverty?

....

....

....

PARENT PAGE

"The King will reply, 'I tell you the truth, whatever you did for one of the least of these brothers of mine, you did for me'" (Matthew 25:40).

Here's an interesting story:

Martin of Tours was a Roman soldier and a Christian. One cold winter day, as he was entering a city, a beggar stopped him and asked of alms; Martin had no money, but the beggar was blue and shivering with cold, and Martin gave what he had. He took off his soldier's coat, worn and frayed as it was; he cut it in two and gave half of it to the beggar man. That night he had a dream. In it he saw the heavenly places and all the angels and Jesus in the midst of them; and Jesus was wearing half a Roman soldier's cloak. One of the angels said to him, "Master, why are you wearing that battered old cloak? Who gave it to you?" And Jesus answered softly, "My servant Martin gave it to me."[1]

The ultimate goal in life is to serve Jesus.

Nobel Peace Prize recipient Mother Teresa of Calcutta, India, was walking the streets of the poorest of poor in Calcutta when a reporter asked her, "What motivated you to commit your life to the sick and dying?" Her reply, "I haven't committed my life to the ill. I've committed my life to Jesus Christ, and it just so happens I see Jesus on the faces of the sick and dying."

If you could serve Jesus in any way possible, what would you do?

....

....

....

What could our family do?

....

....

....

What keeps you from committing your life to the above dream or desire?

....

....

....

Take a few minutes to pray for the needs of the world specifically and by name. Pray also about your partnership in making a difference.

Note

1. William Barclay, *The Gospel of Matthew: The Daily Bible Study Series* (Philadelphia: Westminster Press, 1975), p. 326.

Session 3 "Serving the Poor and Oppressed"
Date ....

SERVANT LEADERS

K EY VERSE

"I have set you an example that you should do as I have done for you."
John 13:15

B IBLICAL BASIS

Mark 10:43-45; John 13:1-20;
2 Peter 3:18

T HE BIG IDEA

Jesus is our example of a servant, and we are to imitate His actions as servant leaders.

A IMS OF THIS SESSION

During this session you will guide students to:

• Examine the concept of servant leadership from the example of Jesus;

• Discover principles of servant leadership found in John 13:1-20;

• Implement a decision to be servant leaders by following the example of Jesus.

W ARM UP

FEET GAMES—

A variety of games played with feet.

T EAM EFFORT— JUNIOR HIGH/ MIDDLE SCHOOL

FROG KISSIN'—

A story about changing into being servant leaders.

T EAM EFFORT— HIGH SCHOOL

A SOLDIER AND A PADRE—

A story on the effects of serving others.

I N THE WORD

A FOOT MEETING—

A Bible study on Jesus' example of serving His followers.

T HINGS TO THINK ABOUT (OPTIONAL)

Questions to get students thinking and talking about servant leadership.

P ARENT PAGE

A tool to get the session into the home and allow parents and young people to discuss how they can be servant leaders to each other.

LEADER'S DEVOTIONAL

"Not so with you. Instead, whoever wants to become great among you must be your servant, and whoever wants to be first must be slave of all. For even the Son of Man did not come to be served, but to serve, and to give his life as a ransom for many" (Mark 10:43-45).

There are a lot of things in this life you most likely won't get rewarded for here on earth. As a Christian and servant leader of Jesus Christ, a lot of your work with young people will probably go unnoticed. You won't hear much applause or see your name in print or find out that you're up for the Nobel Peace Prize. There will be days when you wonder why you spend so much time with teenagers. No one will see when you give Tom a ride home after your youth group meeting for the eighth time in a row. The hours you spend on the phone talking to a kid in crisis won't earn you any frequent listening mileage points. You won't see any trophies for being the youth sponsor of the year. A simple fact of Christian service is that most of your work will, hopefully, go unnoticed. Why? Because that's what being a servant leader is all about.

Jesus talked about not letting your left hand know what your right hand is doing. True greatness in God's kingdom is serving without the need for the praise, approval and recognition of others. It's serving with your eyes on Christ and not yourself. That's not always easy to do. It's natural to want to know that you're making a positive difference in the lives of teenagers. Recognition is the feedback that tells you that you're on target. A simple thank-you is an honest, earthly expression of appreciation. None of those things are wrong; what's important is that we keep recognition in perspective. One thank-you from God will go a lot further than a stadium full of cheering fans. Jesus is your model for giving your life to teenagers. He came to serve and give His life as a ransom for many. As a servant leader, true greatness is waiting for the most important thank-you stored for you in heaven. (Written by Joey O'Connor.)

"If you wish to be a leader you will be frustrated, for very few people wish to be led. If you aim to be a servant you will never be frustrated."—Frank F. Warren

SERVANT LEADERS

KEY VERSE

"I have set you an example that you should do as I have done for you." John 13:15

BIBLICAL BASIS

Mark 10:43-45; John 13:1-20; 2 Peter 3:18

THE BIG IDEA

Jesus is our example of a servant, and we are to imitate His actions as servant leaders.

WARM UP (5-10 MINUTES)

FEET GAMES

• Choose one or more of the following games to play.

1. Shoe relay race: Have all the students take off their shoes. Pile the shoes in the center of the room. Mix up the shoes. Then form relay teams of four people to a team. Let them choose team members with whom they are comfortable. The object of the game is, in a relay race, to find their shoes, put them on and run back to the next person. The team in which everyone has their shoes back on first wins.

2. Foot wrestling: Divide students into pairs. Have pairs sit together without shoes or socks, foot to foot, and lock toes. When the signal is given, students try to "pin" the other persons foot just like in arm wrestling.

3. Foot drawing: Divide students into groups of four. Each team draws a picture using only their feet to draw. Give fun prizes for the most creative, the worst drawing and the most unique.

4. Foot autographs: Divide students into groups of four. Everyone receives a felt-tip marker (the kind that washes off). The group then has two minutes to see how many signatures they can get on their feet.

SO WHAT?

What are specific ways we can humble ourselves and serve others in order to make a difference in their lives?

THINGS TO THINK ABOUT (OPTIONAL)

• Use the questions on page 69 after or as a part of "In the Word."

1. Why does the phrase "servant leadership" seem like words that shouldn't go together?

2. What are illustrations of how Jesus was a servant leader?

3. What are ways this group can be a servant to:

a. our families?

b. our friends?

c. our schools?

d. our church?

e. our neighborhoods?

f. the world?

PARENT PAGE

• Distribute page to parents.

FROG KISSIN'

- Divide students into groups of three or four.
- Give each student a copy of "Frog Kissin'" on page 63 and a pen or pencil, or display a copy using an overhead projector.
- Students complete their pages.

Ever feel like a frog? Frogs feel slow, low, ugly, puffy, drooped, pooped. I know. One told me.

The frog feeling comes when you want to be bright but feel dumb, when you want to be great but are small, when you want to share but you are selfish, when you want to be thankful but feel resentment, when you want to care but are indifferent.

Yes, at one time or another each of us has found him- or herself on a lily pad, floating down the great river of life. Frightened and disgusted, we are too froggish to budge.

Once upon a time there was a frog. But he really wasn't a frog. He was a prince who looked and felt like a frog. A wicked witch had cast a spell on him. Only the kiss of a beautiful maiden could save him. But since when do cute chicks kiss frogs? So there he sat, an unkissed prince in frog form. But miracles happen.

One day a beautiful maiden grabbed him up and gave him a big smack. Crash! Boom! Zap! There he was, a handsome prince. And you know the rest. They lived happily ever after. So what is the task of the Church? To kiss frogs, of course.

1. What do you see as the point of the frog Kissin' story?

2. How does being a servant leader relate to this story?

3. What are specific ways this group can be more effective at servant leadership?

TEAM EFFORT—HIGH SCHOOL

A SOLDIER AND A PADRE (15-20 MINUTES)

- Divide students into groups of three or four.
- Give each student a copy of "A Soldier and a Padre" on page 65 and a pen or pencil, or display a copy using an overhead projector.
- Students complete their pages.

There was a soldier who was wounded in battle. A padre crept over and did what he could for him. He stayed with him when the remainder of the troops retreated. In the heat of the day he gave him water from his own water bottle, while he himself remained parched with thirst. In the night, when the chill frost came down, he covered the wounded man with his own coat, and finally wrapped him up in even more of his own clothes to

save him from the cold. In the end, the wounded man looked up at the padre. Then said the wounded man, "If Christianity makes a man do for another man what you have done for me, tell me about it, because I want it."

1. What do you see as the significance of this story?

2. How does the phrase "If Christianity makes a man do for another man what you have done for me, tell me about it, because I want it" relate to being a servant leader?

3. How can this group be more effective at servant leadership?

IN THE WORD (25-30 MINUTES)

A FOOT MEETING

- Divide students into groups of three or four.
- Give each student a copy of "A Foot Meeting" on page 67 and a pen or pencil, or display a copy using an overhead projector.
- Students complete the Bible study.
- End the Bible study with a feet washing ceremony. Bring out buckets of soapy water and ask each group to wash each others' feet. When finished (and don't worry about it not being a solemn ceremony), ask these questions:
  What makes it uncomfortable to wash others' feet and have your own feet washed?
  Why do you think Jesus washed the disciples' feet?
- Read John 13:1-20.

1. Why do you think Jesus washed His disciples' feet?

2. What lessons did Peter learn from his encounter with Jesus?

3. What is the path of blessing according to John 13:17?

Fold

 **TEAM EFFORT**

FROG KISSIN'

Ever feel like a frog? Frogs feel slow, low, ugly, puffy, drooped, pooped. I know. One told me.

The frog feeling comes when you want to be bright but feel dumb, when you want to share but you are selfish, when you want to be thankful but feel resentment, when you want to be great but are small, when you want to care but are indifferent.

Yes, at one time or another each of us has found him- or herself on a lily pad, floating down the great river of life. Frightened and disgusted, we are too froggish to budge.

Once upon a time there was a frog. But he really wasn't a frog. He was a prince who looked and felt like a frog. A wicked witch had cast a spell on him. Only the kiss of a beautiful maiden could save him. But since when do cute chicks kiss frogs? So there he sat, an unkissed prince in frog form. But miracles happen.

One day a beautiful maiden grabbed him up and gave him a big smack. Crash! Boom! Zap! There he was, a handsome prince. And you know the rest. They lived happily ever after. So what is the task of the Church? To kiss frogs, of course.

I. What do you see as the point of the Frog Kissin' story?

....

....

....

....

....

2. How does being a servant leader relate to this story?

....

....

....

....

....

3. What are specific ways this group can be more effective at servant leadership?

....

....

....

....

TEAM EFFORT

A SOLDIER AND A PADRE

There was a soldier who was wounded in battle. The padre crept over and did what he could for him. He stayed with him when the remainder of the troops retreated. In the heat of the day he gave him water from his own water bottle, while he himself remained parched with thirst. In the night, when the chill frost came down, he covered the wounded man with his own coat, and finally wrapped him up in even more of his own clothes to save him from the cold. In the end, the wounded man looked up at the padre. Then said the wounded man, "If Christianity makes a man do for another man what you have done for me, tell me about it, because I want it." Christianity in action moved him to envy a faith which could produce a life like that.[1]

1. What do you see as the significance of this story?

....

....

....

2. How does the phrase "if Christianity makes a man do for another man what you have done for me, tell me about it, because I want it" relate to being a servant leader?

....

....

....

3. How can this group be more effective at servant leadership?

....

....

....

....

Note

1. William Barclay, *The Letter to Romans: The Daily Bible Study Series, Rev. Ed.* (Philadelphia: Westminster Press, 1975), p. 148.

IN THE WORD

A FOOT MEETING

It was just before the Passover Feast. Jesus knew that the time had come for him to leave this world and go to the Father. Having loved his own who were in the world, he now showed them the full extent of his love.

The evening meal was being served, and the devil had already prompted Judas Iscariot, son of Simon, to betray Jesus. Jesus knew that the Father had put all things under his power, and that he had come from God and was returning to God; so he got up from the meal, took off his outer clothing, and wrapped a towel around his waist. After that, he poured water into a basin and began to wash his disciples' feet, drying them with the towel that was wrapped around him.

He came to Simon Peter, who said to him, "Lord, are you going to wash my feet?"

Jesus replied, "You do not realize now what I am doing, but later you will understand."

"No," said Peter, "you shall never wash my feet."

Jesus answered, "Unless I wash you, you have no part with me."

"Then, Lord," Simon Peter replied, "not just my feet but my hands and my head as well!"

Jesus answered, "A person who has had a bath needs only to wash his feet; his whole body is clean. And you are clean, though not every one of you." For he knew who was going to betray him, and that was why he said not every one was clean.

When he had finished washing their feet, he put on his clothes and returned to his place. "Do you understand what I have done for you?" he asked them. "You call me 'Teacher' and 'Lord,' and rightly so, for that is what I am. Now that I, your Lord and Teacher, have washed your feet, you also should wash one another's feet. I have set you an example that you should do as I have done for you. I tell you the truth, no servant is greater than his master, nor is a messenger greater than the one who sent him. Now that you know these things you will be blessed if you do them.

"I am not referring to all of you; I know those I have chosen. But this is to fulfill the scripture: 'He who shares my bread has lifted up his heel against me.'

"I am telling you now before it happens, so that when it does happen you will believe that am He. I tell you the truth, whoever accepts anyone I send accepts me; and whoever accepts me accepts the one who sent me" (John 13:1-20).

1. Why do you think Jesus washed His disciples' feet?

....

....

2. What lessons did Peter learn from his encounter with Jesus?

....

....

3. What is the path of blessing according to John 13:17?

....

....

SO WHAT?

What are specific ways we can humble ourselves and serve others in order to make a difference in their lives?

....

....

....

....

....

....

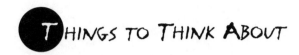 **THINGS TO THINK ABOUT**

1. Why does the phrase "servant leadership" seem like words that shouldn't go together?

....
....
....

2. What are illustrations of how Jesus was a servant leader?

....
....
....

3. What are ways this group can be a servant to:

a. our families?

....
....

b. our friends?

....
....

c. our schools?

....
....

d. our church?

....
....

e. our neighborhoods?

....
....

f. the world?

....
....

 ρARENT ρAGE

ACTIONS SPEAK LOUDER THAN WORDS

"But grow in the grace and knowledge of our Lord and Savior Jesus Christ. To him be glory both now and forever! Amen" (2 Peter 3:18).

How does growing in grace and knowledge of Jesus relate to serving others?

....

....

....

....

What are specific ways we can be servant leaders in the home?

....

....

....

Albert Schweitzer was a person who knew a lot about serving. He was a missionary doctor in Africa. Here's what he had to say about being servant leader: "I don't know what your destiny will be, but one thing I know—the only ones among you who will be truly happy are those who have sought and found how to serve."

Share your impressions of this powerful quote.

....

....

....

How is this quote similar to the statement of Jesus in John 13:12-17?

....

....

....

....

....

Session 4 "Servant Leaders"
Date ....

 71 © 1995 by Gospel Light. Permission to photocopy granted.

Unit II

PEER LEADERSHIP

Leader's Pep Talk

Ministry to students is best done by other students, not by you. One of the most exciting trends in youth ministry today is a move toward a very effective peer-ministry approach to youth work. What we've learned over the years is that students can be leaders and basically, with adult mentoring, they can do most any of the tasks and ministries in youth work.

I see your job in this section as one of building the peer-leadership philosophy into the lives of your students. As they get their priorities straightened out and live lives of integrity, they can be heroic leaders amongst their friends. The peer-leadership traits in this section are life-changing opportunities for your students to catch the vision of being spiritual leaders with their friends. Let's pray we can instill an uncompromising lifestyle of Christian service and integrity into the lives of our students. Challenge your kids to stand above the crowd and lead the way.

As you put these wonderful truths in front of your students, let me remind you of a wonderful verse where I often go for strength:

> He gives strength to the weary and increases the power of
> the weak. Even youths grow tired and weary, and young
> men stumble and fall; but those who hope in the LORD will
> renew their strength. They will soar on wings like eagles;
> they will run and not grow weary, they will walk and not
> be faint (Isaiah 40:29-31).

GETTING YOUR PRIORITIES STRAIGHT

 EY VERSE

"But seek first his kingdom and his righteousness, and all these things will be given to you as well." Matthew 6:33

 IBLICAL BASIS

Matthew 6:25-34; 1 Corinthians 10:31; Colossians 3:17

 HE BIG IDEA

You can make important decisions to get your priorities in line with God's principles.

 IMS OF THIS SESSION

During this session you will guide students to:

• Examine the practical issues of getting their priorities in proper perspective;

• Discover God's priorities for their lives;

• Implement a decision to put God first in their lives.

 ARM UP

IN 30 SECONDS—

Students quickly complete statements about themselves.

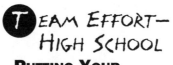 EAM EFFORT— JUNIOR HIGH/ MIDDLE SCHOOL

HOW ARE YOU SPENDING YOUR TIME?—

A look at the average time spent on average activities.

T EAM EFFORT— HIGH SCHOOL

PUTTING YOUR PRIORITIES IN ORDER—

Students prioritize their priorities.

 N THE WORD

PUTTING GOD FIRST—

A Bible study on what it means to put God first in our lives.

 HINGS TO THINK ABOUT (OPTIONAL)

Questions to get students thinking and talking about putting priorities in order.

P ARENT PAGE

A tool to get the session into the home and allow parents and young people to discuss the family priorities.

LEADER'S DEVOTIONAL

"And whatever you do, whether in word or deed, do it all in the name of the Lord Jesus, giving thanks to God the Father through him" (Colossians 3:17).

Whenever I met with prospective youth leaders for our ministry team, I'd ask them two very important questions: 1. What are your most important commitments at this time? 2. What are your most important priorities? Those two questions often seemed to confuse the young, eager people ready to get involved with our youth ministry. Their response, "Well, aren't my commitments and priorities pretty much the same thing?" Well, yes and no.

We all have commitments and we all have priorities. Commitments are the people and tasks we give our time and energy to. Priorities are the way we rank the importance of our commitments. Over the years, I have had a few youth staff members who had a strong commitment to serving students, but who didn't make youth ministry a very high priority with their time schedules. It seemed that their commitments were based upon convenience and not their priorities. To be an effective youth worker, I'd explain to new staff members, there needs to be a clear balance between your commitments and priorities in serving young people.

In youth ministry, as in all of life, your best investment of time will be with your most important commitments. Youth ministry is an area of service that deserves a strong commitment. To be an effective youth worker means making youth ministry a strong commitment and a high priority. That doesn't mean you have to be out five nights a week with teenagers. It simply means taking your ministry seriously, whether it's just sitting down with young people once a week for a Coke or helping to lead a weekly youth event. People who take on too much burn out too quickly. As you serve young people in the name of Jesus, whether a little or a lot, finding a balance between your commitments and priorities can make for an effective, long-term ministry of service. (Written by Joey O'Connor.)

"A man ought to live so that everybody knows he is a Christian...and most of all, his family ought to know."—D.L. Moody

GETTING YOUR PRIORITIES STRAIGHT

KEY VERSE

"But seek first his kingdom and his righteousness, and all these things will be given to you as well." Matthew 6:33

BIBLICAL BASIS

Matthew 6:25-34; 1 Corinthians 10:31; Colossians 3:17

THE BIG IDEA

You can make important decisions to get your priorities in line with God's principles.

WARM UP (5-10 MINUTES)

IN 30 SECONDS

• Divide students into groups of four.
• Have each person in the group complete the following statements in 30 seconds.
  My life story is...
  I feel like...
  My favorite vacation would be...
  One of my most embarrassing moments was...

TEAM EFFORT—JUNIOR HIGH/ MIDDLE SCHOOL (5-10 MINUTES)

HOW ARE YOU SPENDING YOUR TIME?

• Divide students into groups of three or four.
• Give each student a copy of "How Are You Spending Your Time?" on page 79 and a pen or pencil, or display a copy using an overhead projector.
• Students complete their pages.

---- Fold ----

Using Matthew 6:33 and Colossians 3:17, how can you help Laurie?

....

What are other principles to help her get on track with God?

....

SO WHAT?

Given the reality of these Scriptures and the conversations in your group, what growth principles do you need to apply to your own life to get your priorities straight?

....

THINGS TO THINK ABOUT (OPTIONAL)

• Use the questions on page 85 after or as a part of "In the Word."

1. Why do you think it is difficult at times to put our priorities in order?

....

2. What is the most difficult priority for you to put in proper order?

....

3. How can other Christians help you put your priorities in order?

....

PARENT PAGE

• Distribute page to parents.

"So whether you eat or drink or whatever you do, do it all for the glory of God" (1 Corinthians 10:31). The average person, who lives to be 70 years old, will spend:

• 20 years sleeping
• 16 years working
• 7 years playing
• 6 years eating
• 5 years dressing (4½ years for bald-headed men like me!)
• 3 years waiting for somebody
• 1½ years in church
• 1 year on the telephone
• 5 months tying shoes

1. What can you do with your time today that will make a positive difference in your life?

2. What priorities could you develop to help you live life to the fullest?

3. What do 1 Corinthians 10:31 and Colossians 3:17 mean specifically for your life?

TEAM EFFORT—HIGH SCHOOL (15-20 MINUTES)

PUTTING YOUR PRIORITIES IN ORDER

• Divide students into groups of three or four.
• Give each student a copy of "Putting Your Priorities in Order" on page 81 and a pen or pencil, or display a copy using an overhead projector.
• Students complete their pages.

List the 10 most important priorities in your life in the order that you believe they best glorify God.

1.
2.
3.
4.
5.
6.
7.
8.
9.
10.

Why are these your priorities? What makes them important to you?

IN THE WORD (25-30 MINUTES)

PUTTING GOD FIRST

• Divide students into groups of three or four.
• Give each student a copy of "Putting God First" on page 83 and a pen or pencil, or display a copy using an overhead projector.
• Students complete the Bible study.

"But seek first his kingdom and his righteousness, and all these things will be given to you as well" (Matthew 6:33).

Conversation One
Dean: I'm really confused about my faith. I can't seem to get my priorities straight.
Cristy: You're not alone. We all feel that way at times.
Dean: I just wish there was an easy answer, or I'd get a handwritten message from God telling me what to do.
Cristy: We do have the Bible, ya' know.
Dean: I know, but it's confusing, and I've heard it's even controversial.
Cristy: Have you ever read it?
Dean: Not really. I really do want to put God first in my life.
Cristy: Then why don't you look at what Jesus said about putting God first.
Dean: Okay. Where do I start?
Cristy: Read Matthew 6:25-34.

Read Matthew 6:25-34.
With Matthew 6:33 in mind, what are Dean's issues?

What's it going to take for Dean to put God first?

Conversation Two
Laurie: You just don't understand. I do try to get my priorities straight and live for God.
Herb: What's holding you back?
Laurie: I don't know. I just don't feel God's presence in my life very often.
Herb: You know, Laurie, doing some of the stuff you do isn't going to help in getting your spiritual life together.
Laurie: I know, Herb, but it's really difficult.
Herb: Nobody said it would be easy. Let me give you a few suggestions to help turn your life toward God and walk in His ways.

HOW ARE YOU SPENDING YOUR TIME?

"So whether you eat or drink or whatever you do, do it all for the glory of God" (1 Corinthians 10:31).

The average person, who lives to be 70 years old, will spend:

- 20 years sleeping
- 16 years working
- 7 years playing
- 6 years eating
- 5 years dressing (4½ years for bald-headed men like me!)
- 3 years waiting for somebody
- 1½ years in church
- 1 year on the telephone
- 5 months tying shoes

1. What can you do with your time today that will make a positive difference in your life?

....

....

....

2. What priorities could you develop to help you live life to the fullest?

....

....

....

3. What do 1 Corinthians 10:31 and Colossians 3:17 mean specifically for your life?

....

....

....

....

TEAM EFFORT

PUTTING YOUR PRIORITIES IN ORDER

List the 10 most important priorities in your life in the order that you believe they best glorify God.

1. ....

2. ....

3. ....

4. ....

5. ....

6. ....

7. ....

8. ....

9. ....

10. ....

Why are these your priorities? What makes them important to you?

....

....

....

....

....

....

....

....

....

....

....

....

....

....

....

....

IN THE WORD

PUTTING GOD FIRST

"But seek first his kingdom and his righteousness, and all these things will be given to you as well" (Matthew 6:33).

Conversation One

Dean: I'm really confused about my faith. I can't seem to get my priorities straight.

Cristy: You're not alone. We all feel that way at times.

Dean: I just wish there was an easy answer, or I'd get a handwritten message from God telling me what to do.

Cristy: We do have the Bible, ya' know.

Dean: I know, but it's confusing, and I've heard it's even controversial.

Cristy: Have you ever read it?

Dean: Not really. I really do want to put God first in my life.

Cristy: Then why don't you look at what Jesus said about putting God first.

Dean: Okay. Where do I start?

Cristy: Read Matthew 6:25-34.

Read Matthew 6:25-34.

With Matthew 6:33 in mind, what are Dean's issues?

....

....

What's it going to take for Dean to put God first?

....

Conversation Two

Laurie: You just don't understand. I do try to get my priorities straight and live for God.

Herb: What's holding you back?

Laurie: I don't know. I just don't feel God's presence in my life very often.

Herb: You know, Laurie, doing some of the stuff you do isn't going to help in getting your spiritual life together.

Laurie: I know, Herb, but it's really difficult.

Herb: Nobody said it would be easy. Let me give you a few suggestions to help turn your life toward God and walk in His ways.

Using Matthew 6:33 and Colossians 3:17, how can you help Laurie?

....

....

What are other principles to help her get on track with God?

....

....

SO WHAT?

Given the reality of these Scriptures and the conversations in your group, what growth principles do you need to apply to your own life to get your priorities straight?

....

....

....

....

....

....

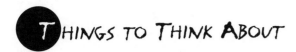

THINGS TO THINK ABOUT

1. Why do you think it is difficult at times to put our priorities in order?

....

....

....

....

....

2. What is the most difficult priority for you to put in proper order?

....

....

....

....

....

....

3. How can other Christians help you put your priorities in order?

....

....

....

....

....

....

....

....

....

PARENT PAGE

LIFE PRIORITIES

Listed below are 15 items. Your job as a family is to rank each priority in order, with 1 being the highest priority and 15 being the lowest priority.

.... Having a wonderful family life without any hassles

.... Walking closely with God

.... Being physically attractive

.... Knowing God's will

.... Being a great athlete

.... Having all the money we need to be happy

.... Serving others

.... Reading the Bible and praying daily

.... Owning a beautiful home

.... Owning a vacation home

.... Never having pimples

.... Never being sick

.... Having close friendships

.... Getting good grades

.... Having a real hunger to live for God

Session 5 "Getting Your Priorities Straight"

Date ....

HEROIC LEADERSHIP

K EY VERSE

"I can do everything through him who gives me strength." Philippians 4:13

B IBLICAL BASIS

1 Samuel 17:1-58; Ephesians 3:20,21; Philippians 4:13

T HE BIG IDEA

You can do something heroic for Jesus Christ as you realize He is your strength.

A IMS OF THIS SESSION

During this session you will guide students to:

• Examine what it would take to do something great for God;

• Discover their dreams and desires to make a difference in the world;

• Implement a plan to achieve their dreams and go for it with God.

W ARM UP

MOST-ADMIRED LIST—

Students list who they admire and why.

T EAM EFFORT— JUNIOR HIGH/ MIDDLE SCHOOL

YOU DON'T HAVE TO BE AVERAGE—

A story of knowing who you are in Christ.

T EAM EFFORT— HIGH SCHOOL

DO SOMETHING HEROIC—

A story on the hero potential.

I N THE WORD

A PINT-SIZED HERO—

A Bible study on being heroic for Jesus.

T HINGS TO THINK ABOUT (OPTIONAL)

Questions to get students thinking and talking about being heroic.

P ARENT PAGE

A tool to get the session into the home and allow parents and young people to discuss who they desire to be for God.

Leader's Devotional

"Now to him who is able to do immeasurably more than all we ask or imagine, according to his power that is at work within us, to him be glory in the church and in Christ Jesus throughout all generations, for ever and ever! Amen" (Ephesians 3:20,21).

One of my youth ministry heroes is a high school volunteer named Ryan. Ryan is a college student with an incredible enthusiasm for Jesus and who loves kids tremendously. The reason why Ryan inspires me so much is his attitude about young people. He is convinced that teenagers need to discover the incredible love of God and he'll do anything to be a positive influence in student's lives. Ryan takes kids surfing, teaches them how to snorkel and leads a small-group Bible study at his house called "The Shack."

Years earlier, when Ryan was in high school, he only came to our youth ministry a few times. Girls, volleyball and the party scene were more important to him than God. Then, when he got into college, he finally sensed a deeper need for something more. After giving his life to Christ, he's never been the same. Ryan has committed himself to serving young people and influencing them toward a personal relationship with God. He's the type of hero that inspires me to be all that God has called me to be.

Like Ryan, you have the powerful opportunity to be a hero for God's kingdom. It is God working through you to do immeasurably more than you could ever ask or imagine in the lives of the students you serve. Because of your love for young people, the living God will use you to communicate the compassion of Jesus. Your enthusiasm for Jesus Christ will demonstrate the concrete reality of God to students who question His existence. Just as Ryan wasn't very interested in God during high school and later made a commitment to Christ, never underestimate God's power to change a student's life even if he or she only comes to your group two or three times. Even if the students in your youth ministry never tell you so, then hear it from me: You are a hero for Jesus Christ. (Written by Joey O'Connor.)

"Leader...a person with a God-given capacity and a God-given responsibility to influence a specific group of God's people toward His purposes for the group."— Bobby Clinton

HEROIC LEADERSHIP

KEY VERSE

"I can do everything through him who gives me strength." Philippians 4:13

BIBLICAL BASIS

1 Samuel 17:1-58; Ephesians 3:20,21; Philippians 4:13

THE BIG IDEA

You can do something heroic for Jesus Christ as you realize He is your strength.

WARM UP (5-10 Minutes)

MOST-ADMIRED LIST

• Give each student a copy of "Most-Admired List" on page 93 and a pen or pencil, or display a copy using an overhead projector.

• Students individually complete their pages.

List 5 to 10 people for your most-admired list.

1.
2.
3.
4.
5.
6.
7.
8.
9.
10.

What do you most admire about these people?

Fold

Are there any other insights from this story?

Is there a "Goliath" in your life that keeps you from being more than average? If so, what is it?

What do you need to do to slay your Goliath?

Here are a few questions to help you along the way of pursuing your dreams;
1. Do you care about the things of the world more than you care about Jesus?
2. Do you love Jesus enough to say NO to the world's standards?
3. Are you willing to lose all prestige to follow the call of God?
4. Is your goal in life to be known (be rich) or to follow Jesus?
5. Are you willing to pay the price of faithfulness?
Too many Christians remain comfortable and stagnant when they could do something heroic for Jesus

SO WHAT?

What would it take to really become all that God intends you to become?

What's holding you back?
____ Fear
____ Lack of faith
____ Peer pressure
____ Lack of desire
____ Lack of maturity
____ Spiritual questions
____ Other
May your prayers be that you will settle for nothing less than heroism. GO FOR IT!

THINGS TO THINK ABOUT (OPTIONAL)

• Use the questions on page 101 after or as a part of "In the Word."
1. Why do you think people settle for second-best in their lives?

2. How can using the gifts God has given you make you a hero for God?

3. How can we as fellow Christians challenge each other to become heroes for Christ?

PARENT PAGE

• Distribute page to parents.

Which of these people would you like to be like and why?

What would be action steps to becoming the kind of leader God wants you to be?

TEAM EFFORT—JUNIOR HIGH/ MIDDLE SCHOOL

YOU DON'T HAVE TO BE AVERAGE (15-20 MINUTES)

- Divide students into groups of three or four.
- Give each student a copy of "You Don't Have to Be Average" on page 95 and a pen or pencil, or display a copy using an overhead projector.
- Students complete their pages.

There are too many people today who settle for second-best in life. Mediocrity is all they put into life, and mediocrity is all they get out of life. Yet Paul said, "I can do all things through Christ who strengthens me" (Philippians 4:13, NKJV). He doesn't sound like a person who chooses to be average and you don't have to be average either.

An American Indian legend tells about a brave who found an eagle's egg and put it into the nest of a prairie chicken. The eaglet hatched with the brood of chicks and grew up with them.

All his life, the changeling eagle—thinking he was a prairie chicken—did what the prairie chickens did. He scratched in the dirt for seeds and insects to eat. He clucked and cackled. And he flew in a brief thrashing of wings and flurry of feathers no more than a few feet off the ground. After all, that's how prairie chickens were supposed to fly.

Years passed. And the changeling eagle grew very old. One day, he saw a magnificent bird far above him in the cloudless sky. Hanging with graceful majesty on the powerful wind currents, it soared with scarcely a beat of its strong golden wings.

"What a beautiful bird!" said the changeling eagle to his neighbor. "What is it?"

"That's an eagle. The chief of the birds," the neighbor clucked. "But don't give it a second thought. You could never be like him."

So the changeling eagle never gave it another thought. And it died thinking it was a prairie chicken.

What was the tragedy of the story?

How does this story relate to your life?

"I can do everything through him who gives me strength" (Philippians 4:13). How can these 10 words change your life?

If you could really do anything you wanted in Christ, what would you do?

- - - - Fold - - - -

TEAM EFFORT—HIGH SCHOOL (15-20 MINUTES)

DO SOMETHING HEROIC

- Divide students into groups of three or four.
- Give each student a copy of "Do Something Heroic" on page 97 and a pen or pencil, or display a copy using an overhead projector.
- Students complete their pages.

A great philosopher tells us about a make-believe country where only ducks live. On Sunday morning all the ducks came into church, waddled down the aisle, waddled into the pews, and squatted. Then the duck minister came in, took his place behind the pulpit, opened the Duck Bible and read, "Ducks! You have wings, and with wings, you can fly like eagles. You can soar into the sky! Ducks! You have wings!" All the ducks yelled, "Amen!" and then they all waddled home.

Many Christians are like those ducks. They know the truth but they don't act upon the truth. They are unhappy because they've settled for mediocrity.

You can do something heroic in Jesus! You can be a hero for Jesus.

As you were growing up, who were your heroes? Why?

Who are your heroes today?

From a Christian perspective, heroes are not always famous or successful. Heroes are faithful. God is not looking for superstars. He is looking for faithful men and women.

What (if anything) is holding you back?

If you could do anything with your life, what would it be?

IN THE WORD (25-30 MINUTES)

A PINT-SIZED HERO

- Divide students into groups of three or four.
- Give each student a copy of "A Pint-Sized Hero" on page 99 and a pen or pencil, or display a copy using an overhead projector.
- Students complete the Bible study.

The Story of David and Goliath
Read 1 Samuel 17:1-58.

In the conversation between David and Saul in verses 31-37, why is David confident in his fight with Goliath?

What motivated David to stand up to the 9½-foot giant? Look carefully at verses 26,36,45-47.

MOST-ADMIRED LIST
List 5 to 10 people for your most-admired list.

1. ....
2. ....
3. ....
4. ....
5. ....
6. ....
7. ....
8. ....
9. ....
10. ....

What do you most admire about these people?

....

....

....

Which of these people would you like to be like and why?

....

....

....

....

What would be action steps to becoming the kind of leader God wants you to be?

....

....

....

....

....

TEAM EFFORT

YOU DON'T HAVE TO BE AVERAGE

There are too many people today who settle for second-best in life. Mediocrity is all they put into life, and mediocrity is all they get out of life. Yet Paul said, "I can do all things through Christ who strengthens me" (Philippians 4:13, *NKJV*). He doesn't sound like a person who chooses to be average and you don't have to be average either.

An American Indian legend tells about a brave who found an eagle's egg and put it into the nest of a prairie chicken. The eaglet hatched with the brood of chicks and grew up with them.

All his life, the changeling eagle—thinking he was a prairie chicken—did what the prairie chickens did.

He scratched in the dirt for seeds and insects to eat. He clucked and cackled. And he flew in a brief thrashing of wings and flurry of feathers no more than a few feet off the ground. After all, that's how prairie chickens were supposed to fly.

Years passed. And the changeling eagle grew very old. One day, he saw a magnificent bird far above him in the cloudless sky. Hanging with graceful majesty on the powerful wind currents, it soared with scarcely a beat of its strong golden wings.

"What a beautiful bird!" said the changeling eagle to his neighbor. "What is it?"

"That's an eagle. The chief of the birds," the neighbor clucked. "But don't give it a second thought. You could never be like him."

So the changeling eagle never gave it another thought. And it died thinking it was a prairie chicken.[1]

What was the tragedy of the story?

....

....

How does this story relate to your life?

....

....

"I can do everything through him who gives me strength" (Philippians 4:13). How can these 10 words change your life?

....

....

If you could really do or be anything you wanted in Christ, what would you do?

....

....

....

Note

1. "The Changeling Eagle," *Christopher News Notes,* no. 229.

TEAM EFFORT

DO SOMETHING HEROIC

A great philosopher tells us about a make-believe country where only ducks live. On Sunday morning all the ducks came into church, waddled down the aisle, waddled into the pews, and squatted. Then the duck minister came in, took his place behind the pulpit, opened the Duck Bible and read, "Ducks! You have wings, and with wings, you can fly like eagles. You can soar into the sky! Ducks! You have wings!" All the ducks yelled "Amen!" and then they all waddled home.[1]

Many Christians are like those ducks. They know the truth but they don't act upon the truth. They are unhappy because they've settled for mediocrity!

You can do something heroic for Jesus! You can be a hero for Jesus.

As you were growing up, who were your heroes? Why?

....

....

....

Who are your heroes today?

....

....

From a Christian perspective, heroes are not always famous or successful. Heroes are faithful. God is not looking for superstars. He is looking for faithful men and women.

If you could do anything with your life, what would it be?

....

....

....

What (if anything) is holding you back?

....

....

....

....

Note

1. Tony Campolo, *You Can Make a Difference* (Dallas: Word Books, 1984), p. 74.

IN THE WORD

A PINT-SIZED HERO
The Story of David and Goliath

Read 1 Samuel 17:1-58.

In the conversation between David and Saul in verses 31-37, why is David confident in his fight with Goliath?

....

....

What motivated David to stand up to the 9½-foot giant? Look carefully at verses 26,36,45-47.

....

....

Are there any other insights from this story?

....

....

Is there a "Goliath" in your life that keeps you from being more than average? If so, what is it?

....

....

What do you need to do to slay your Goliath?

....

....

Here are a few questions to help you along the way of pursuing your dreams:

1. Do you care about the things of the world more than you care about Jesus?

....

2. Do you love Jesus enough to say NO to the world's standards?

....

3. Are you willing to lose all prestige to follow the call of God?

....

4. Is your goal in life to be known (be rich) or to follow Jesus?

....

5. Are you willing to pay the price of faithfulness?

....

Too many Christians remain comfortable and stagnant when they could do something heroic for Jesus.

SO WHAT?
What would it take to really become all that God intends you to become?

....

....

....

....

....

What's holding you back?
.... Fear
.... Lack of faith
.... Peer pressure
.... Lack of desire
.... Lack of maturity
.... Spiritual questions
.... Other ....

May your prayers be that you will settle for nothing less than heroism. GO FOR IT!

THINGS TO THINK ABOUT

1. Why do you think people settle for second-best in their lives?

....
....
....
....
....
....

2. How can using the gifts God has given you make you a hero for God?

....
....
....
....
....
....
....

3. How can we as fellow Christians challenge each other to become heroes for Christ?

....
....
....
....
....
....
....
....
....
....

PARENT PAGE

GO FOR IT

"I can do everything through him who gives me strength" (Philippians 4:13).

Let's Pretend...

If you could become any type of person you wanted to become with the wave of a magic wand, who would you want to become? **Write or share a short description. Here are a few areas you might want to consider:**

Personality   Relationship with God
Actions   Relationships with others
Lifestyle   Family relationships
Career

....
....
....
....

Share what keeps you from "going for it" when it comes to the above areas.

....
....
....
....
....

What do you need from your family, friends and church to not settle for mediocrity but choose to "go for it" for God?

....
....
....
....
....
....
....

Session 6 "Heroic Leadership"

Date...

INTEGRITY

 KEY VERSE

"Blessed are the pure in heart, for they will see God." Matthew 5:8

BIBLICAL BASIS

Genesis 39:1-23; Psalm 78:72; Proverbs 2:1-15,20-22; 10:9; 28:18; Daniel 6:1-24; Matthew 5:8; Luke 6:31; Galatians 5:16; Ephesians 4:18,19; Colossians 3:9,10; 2 Timothy 2:22; Hebrews 4:13; 1 John 1:6

THE BIG IDEA

God desires us to become people who are trustworthy, honest and wise. A lifestyle of integrity leads to a fulfilled and happy life.

AIMS OF THIS SESSION

During this session you will guide students to:

• Examine biblical stories of a life of integrity;

• Discover the principles of a life of integrity;

• Implement a lifestyle of integrity, purity and honesty in their faith and actions.

 WARM UP

TWO TRUTHS AND A LIE—

Students learn the truth about each other.

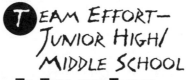 TEAM EFFORT— JUNIOR HIGH/ MIDDLE SCHOOL

TO TELL THE TRUTH—

A game show that deals with telling the truth.

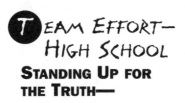 TEAM EFFORT— HIGH SCHOOL

STANDING UP FOR THE TRUTH—

Students discuss what they think integrity is.

 IN THE WORD

THE INTEGRITY OF GOD'S PEOPLE—

A Bible study on two men of integrity.

THINGS TO THINK ABOUT (OPTIONAL)

Questions to get students thinking and talking about what it means to be a person of integrity.

PARENT PAGE

A tool to get the session into the home and allow parents and young people to discuss honesty, purity and wisdom.

LEADER'S DEVOTIONAL

"And David shepherded them with integrity of heart; with skillful hands he led them" (Psalm 78:72).

Ky is one of the students in the high school ministry at my church. One day Ky and Todd, the high school pastor, were talking and Todd asked Ky what his dad did for work.

"Oh, he's a lawyer," Ky replied.

"What kind of lawyer?" Todd responded.

Ky looked Todd in the face and declared, "The kind that's never home."

Ky's family lives in the most expensive area in town. They have a huge home with carpet so thick it feels like you're walking on soft pillows. Ky has a nice truck, a drumset and all sorts of other fun toys, but that stuff doesn't really matter to him. Ky doesn't care what his dad does for work; all he wishes for is a dad to spend time with him. Just a normal relationship with his dad—that's all Ky really wants.

Young people today are looking for adults to lead them with integrity. Teenagers know integrity when they see it and they know it when they don't. Absent parents, broken promises, lies and hypocritical ways of living are the thin masks students see right through to adults who claim to be something they're not. Young people can smell hypocrisy from a mile away. What they want are people of integrity and adults who really care about them.

The Bible says that David shepherded his people with integrity of heart and led them with skillful hands. Integrity of heart is living according to God's principles in everything you do. It's living on the outside who God is making you to be on the inside. That's the demonstration of godly living young people are searching for. They want a demonstration of the gospel first, then an explanation. You may not be able to give your students everything they want, but by living a life of integrity, you'll be giving them an authentic, godly example of following Christ. And that's something they really need! (Written by Joey O'Connor.)

"Integrity is living on the outside who you are on the inside."

INTEGRITY

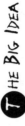

KEY VERSE

"Blessed are the pure in heart, for they will see God." Matthew 5:8

BIBLICAL BASIS

Genesis 39:1-23; Psalm 78:72; Proverbs 2:1-15,20-22; 10:9; 28:18; Daniel 6:1-24; Matthew 5:8; Luke 6:31; Galatians 5:16; Ephesians 4:18,19; Colossians 3:9,10; 2 Timothy 2:22; Hebrews 4:13; 1 John 1:6

THE BIG IDEA

God desires us to become people who are trustworthy, honest and wise. A lifestyle of integrity leads to a fulfilled and happy life.

WARM UP (5-10 MINUTES)

TWO TRUTHS AND A LIE

• Divide students into groups of three or four.

• Have each person tell two truths and one lie about him- or herself. When each member has finished, have the group guess which were the lies.

TEAM EFFORT—JUNIOR HIGH/MIDDLE SCHOOL (15-20 MINUTES)

TO TELL THE TRUTH

• Before class, choose three contestants. Make sure one has an unusual or humorous personal account to tell. Then choose two others who will lie.

• Only one of the contestants will be telling the truth. For example: First person: Hi, I'm Jim Burns, and I threw up on my first date. Next person: Hi, I'm Gary Lenhart, and I threw up on my first date. Next person: Hi, I'm Luchi Bierbower, and I threw up on my first date.

• Have students ask each contestant any question they want. After a few minutes they have

--- Fold ---

Characteristic	How to Improve It
1.	
2.	
3.	
4.	
5.	

THINGS TO THINK ABOUT (OPTIONAL)

• Use the questions on page 113 after or as a part of "In the Word."

1. Write out your own definition of integrity, and share ways you can develop more integrity in your own life.

2. Why is it difficult to find people of integrity?

3. Read I John 1:6. Would you consider this type of person a person of integrity? Why or why not?

PARENT PAGE

• Distribute page to parents.

to guess who was lying and who was telling the truth. Then say as the TV show said, "Will the real person who threw up on his or her first date please stand up?"

- Then ask these questions:
  1. Is there such a thing as a white lie?
  2. Is dishonesty ever justifiable?
  3. Give an example of dishonesty in school, family, church and government.

TEAM EFFORT—HIGH SCHOOL (15-20 MINUTES)

STANDING UP FOR THE TRUTH

- Create a "Strongly Agree" sign, an "Agree" sign, an "Undecided" sign, a "Disagree" sign and a "Strongly Disagree" sign. Place the five signs at different locations throughout the room.
- After each of the following statements are read, the students are to move to whatever sign most clearly represents what they believe. Then let each section tell why they voted the way they did.
  1. God wants us to always tell the truth.
  2. The majority of people are mainly people of integrity.
  3. Pastors have more integrity than politicians.
  4. If a store clerk gives you back too much change and you are already at home, you should always go back to the store and give the extra money to the clerk.

IN THE WORD (25-30 MINUTES)

THE INTEGRITY OF GOD'S PEOPLE

- Divide students into groups of three or four.
- Give each student a copy of "The Integrity of God's People" on pages 109-111 and a pen or pencil, or display a copy using an overhead projector.
- Students complete the Bible study.

One of the greatest compliments you could ever receive is to be called a woman or man of integrity. People of integrity can be trusted. People of integrity are honest. People of integrity have pure motives. Let's meet two people in the Old Testament who were men of integrity.

Daniel
Read Daniel 6:1-24 and answer the following questions about this story. As you get better acquainted with Daniel, you'll see why he was a man of integrity.

Verse 3: Why was Daniel distinguished above all the other leaders?
....

Verse 4: What happened when Daniel's fellow leaders tried to find fault in him?
....

Verse 10: What did Daniel do after King Darius signed the document?
....

Fold

Verse 14: Why do you think the king was distressed when he heard from the other leaders that Daniel had remained faithful to his God?
....

Verses 16-18: What was the king's desire concerning Daniel's life in the lions' den?
....

Verses 19-24: What were the results of Daniel's integrity and faithfulness to God?
....

Joseph
For another look at a man of integrity, take some time in the next few days to read about Joseph, Genesis 37–50. In Joseph we see a person who was betrayed by his very own brothers. Yet, in the end, Joseph saved his family from starvation.
Time after time in this story we see God abundantly blessing Joseph because of his honesty and integrity. Let's look at one episode in the life of Joseph. Read Genesis 39:1-23.

Verses 1-6: Why did Potiphar leave Joseph in charge of everything in his house and field?
....

Verses 7-10: What was Joseph's response to the plea of his master's wife?
....

Verses 11,12: What did Joseph do when Potiphar's wife cornered him in the house?
....

Verses 13-18: Why do you suppose Potiphar's wife lied about Joseph?
....

Verses 19-23: How did Joseph act in prison?
....

Verse 21: What was God's response to Joseph's integrity?
....

So WHAT?

Take a personal-integrity inventory. List the issues and characteristics in your life that are lacking integrity. Then beside each one, make a note of how you can improve this quality in your life.
....

IN THE WORD

THE INTEGRITY OF GOD'S PEOPLE

One of the greatest compliments you could ever receive is to be called a woman or man of integrity. People of integrity can be trusted. People of integrity are honest. People of integrity have pure motives. Let's meet two people in the Old Testament who were men of integrity.

Daniel

Read Daniel 6:1-24 and answer the following questions about this story. As you get better acquainted with Daniel, you'll see why he was a man of integrity.

Verse 3: Why was Daniel distinguished above all the other leaders?

....

....

Verse 4: What happened when Daniel's fellow leaders tried to find fault in him?

....

....

Verse 10: What did Daniel do after King Darius signed the document?

....

....

....

Verse 14: Why do you think the king was distressed when he heard from the other leaders that Daniel had remained faithful to his God?

....

....

Verses 16-18: What was the king's desire concerning Daniel's life in the lions' den?

....

....

Verses 19-24: What were the results of Daniel's integrity and faithfulness to God?

....

....

....

 **N THE WORD**

Joseph

For another look at a man of integrity, take some time in the next few days to read about Joseph, Genesis 37—50. In Joseph we see a person who was betrayed by his very own brothers. Yet, in the end, Joseph saved his family from starvation.

Time after time in this story we see God abundantly blessing Joseph because of his honesty and integrity. Let's look at one episode in the life of Joseph. Read Genesis 39:1-23.

Verses 1-6: Why did Potiphar leave Joseph in charge of everything in his house and field?

....

....

Verses 7-10: What was Joseph's response to the plea of his master's wife?

....

....

Verses 11,12: What did Joseph do when Potiphar's wife cornered him in the house?

....

....

Verses 13-18: Why do you suppose Potiphar's wife lied about Joseph?

....

....

Verses 19-23: How did Joseph act in prison?

....

....

Verse 21: What was God's response to Joseph's integrity?

....

So What?

Take a personal-integrity inventory. List the issues and characteristics in your life that are lacking integrity. Then beside each one, make a note of how you can improve this quality in your life.

Characteristic	How to Improve It
1.	
2.	
3.	
4.	
5.	

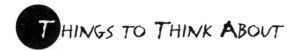 HINGS TO THINK ABOUT

1. Write out your own definition of integrity, and share ways you can develop more integrity in your own life.

....
....
....
....
....

2. Why is it difficult to find people of integrity?

....
....
....
....
....

3. Read 1 John 1:6. Would you consider this type of person a person of integrity? Why or why not?

....
....
....
....
....
....
....
....
....
....
....

PARENT PAGE

On as scale of 1 to 10, with 10 being the highest and 1 being the lowest, how would you rate yourself in these traits of integrity?

.... Honesty
.... Purity
.... Wisdom

Honesty

According to Colossians 3:9,10, why should we not lie to one another?

....

....

How does Luke 6:31 reflect the idea of living honestly?

....

....

Read Hebrews 4:13. Why is it useless to try to deceive God?

....

....

Purity

What does Jesus say about the pure in heart in Matthew 5:8?

....

....

How did Paul describe those who practice impurity in Ephesians 4:18,19?

....

....

What suggestions does Paul give us in these verses on how to live a pure life?

Galatians 5:16

....

....

2 Timothy 2:22

....

....

PARENT PAGE

Wisdom

Read Proverbs 2:1-15. List a few of the rewards for seeking wisdom.

....
....
....
....

What can you personally do to develop the characteristic of wisdom in your life?

....
....
....

The book of Proverbs is said to be "words to the wise." Read these verses and then write what they have to say about integrity.
Proverbs 2:20-22

....
....

Proverbs 10:9

....
....

Proverbs 28:18

....
....

How can we as a family become more of a family of integrity?

....
....
....
....
....
....

Session 7 "Integrity"

Date..

FRIENDSHIP: A PRICELESS GIFT

KEY VERSE

"A friend loves at all times, and a brother is born for adversity."
Proverbs 17:17

BIBLICAL BASIS

1 Samuel 20:17,42; Proverbs 17:17; Ecclesiastes 4:8-12; John 15:12,13,15; Romans 12:15; 1 Corinthians 13:4; Galatians 6:2

THE BIG IDEA

True friendship brings out the best in people. Friendship is an incredible gift from God.

AIMS OF THIS SESSION

During this session you will guide students to:
• Examine characteristics of a true friend;
• Discover what characteristics of friendship will be important in their lives;
• Implement practical changes using the true qualities of friendship to improve their relationships with others.

WARM UP

COMMON BONDS—
A look at the similarities in students.

TEAM EFFORT— JUNIOR HIGH/ MIDDLE SCHOOL

A PRICELESS GIFT—
Students reflect on their friendships.

TEAM EFFORT— HIGH SCHOOL

FRIENDSHIP SURVEY SHEET—
A survey of students' friendships.

IN THE WORD

A TRUE FRIEND—
A Bible study on being a true friend.

THINGS TO THINK ABOUT (OPTIONAL)

Questions to get students thinking and talking about God's purpose in friendships.

PARENT PAGE

A tool to get the session into the home and allow parents and young people to discuss their friendships.

LEADER'S DEVOTIONAL

"I no longer call you servants, because a servant does not know his master's business. Instead, I have called you friends, for everything that I learned from my Father I have made known to you" (John 15:15).

The other day my wife, Krista, and I went to a bagel shop for breakfast, and we happened to bump into a girl who used to be involved in our youth ministry. The girl's name was Kim and in high school, she hung out with a fun gang of friends—Misty, Heather, Lori, Kristen, Brian, Danny and Ryan. Most of those students had never gone to church before, but as a group, they went on trip after trip with our outreach ministry.

Kim was now in college and we asked her if she still hung out with the old gang. With a sad look on her face, she dropped her smile and said, "No, none of us spend time together anymore. The gang's no longer a gang. We've all kind of gone our separate ways."

Krista and I talked to Kim a little bit more and finally said good-bye. Afterwards, Krista and I discussed how amazing it is when friendships change after high school. In our estimation, Kim didn't seem to be the fun, friendly, bubbly high school girl we used to know. It was obvious by the tone of her voice and the look on her face that Kim was lonelier than she'd ever been before.

Teaching young people friendship with God is the most priceless gift you can give them. A lot of teenagers think that their junior high and high school friends will be friends for life. Unfortunately, we know that's not always true.

But, a friendship with Jesus Christ can last for eternity. When young people discover that Jesus offers His friendship to them, they'll never have to be friendless again. By being a friend to young people, you also have the opportunity to introduce them to your Best Friend, Jesus Christ. You are a critical bridge to teenagers discovering the most wonderful Friend of all. (Written by Joey O'Connor.)

"A friend is a person with whom you dare to be yourself."—William Shakespeare

FRIENDSHIP: A PRICELESS GIFT

KEY VERSE

"A friend loves at all times, and a brother is born for adversity." Proverbs 17:17

BIBLICAL BASIS

1 Samuel 20:17,42; Proverbs 17:17; Ecclesiastes 4:8-12; John 15:12,13,15; Romans 12:15; 1 Corinthians 13:4; Galatians 6:2

THE BIG IDEA

True friendship brings out the best in people. Friendship is an incredible gift from God.

WARM UP (5-10 MINUTES)

COMMON BONDS

- Divide students into pairs.
- Tell them they have three minutes to find as many things as possible that they have in common. The students can write the similarities on a piece of paper. Remind them they can't say things like we both have a nose, eyes, etc. Have a contest for the most things in common and the most unique thing found in common.
- Give prizes for the most things in common and the most unique thing found in common.

TEAM EFFORT—JUNIOR HIGH/ MIDDLE SCHOOL (15-20 MINUTES)

A PRICELESS GIFT

- Divide students into groups of three or four.
- Give each student a copy of "A Priceless Gift" on page 123 and a pen or pencil, or display a copy using an overhead projector.
- Students complete their pages.

There are very few things in life as important or as wonderful as true friendship. A good friend is a treasure beyond almost anything else in life. Friendship is a priceless gift from God. Take a moment to reflect on your friendships.

What are little everyday sacrifices that w

How do you think this Scripture relates t

4. Patient
"Love is patient" (1 Corinthians 13:4).
Why do you suppose patience is include

Think of a friend with whom you can be with him or her.

5. A Good Listener
It has been said that listening is the language of love. Who listens to you?

How has his or her listening influenced your life in a positive way?

Is this quality a strength or a weakness in your life? If it's a weakness, how can you become a better listener? If it is already a strength, congratulations! You, no doubt, are a positive influence in somebody's life!

So What?
Now that you have investigated the true qualities of a friend, what practical changes can you make in your friendships?

THINGS TO THINK ABOUT (OPTIONAL)

- Use the questions on page 131 after or as a part of "In the Word."
1. Why do you think God gives us friends?

2. True friendship is costly. What do you think it takes to develop a deeper friendship?

3. Read Ecclesiastes 4:8-12. How do these verses relate to friendship?

PARENT PAGE
- Distribute page to parents.

Leilani has permission to view the film "Passion of the Christ" with her Sunday School Class.

Chuck Jones

List three people you consider to be true friends. Why?

1.
2.
3.

List the names of three to five people with whom you would like to become better friends.

1.
2.
3.
4.
5.

TEAM EFFORT—HIGH SCHOOL (15-20 Minutes)

FRIENDSHIP SURVEY SHEET

• Divide students into groups of three or four.
• Give each student a copy of "Friendship Survey Sheet" on page 125 and a pen or pencil, or display a copy using an overhead projector.
• Students complete their pages.

1. How many friends do you have?
2. Do you have friends of both sexes?
3. Do you have friends who are five years younger than you?
4. Do you have friends who are five years older than you?
5. What's the craziest thing you've done with friends?
6. Who would consider you one of their friends?
7. List three qualities you have that make you a good friend.
8. What qualities does your best friend have?
9. Are your parents your friends? Why or why not?
10. Do you have more or fewer friends than you had one year ago?
11. Are you a good friend? Why?

IN THE WORD (25-30 Minutes)

A TRUE FRIEND

• Divide students into groups of three or four.
• Give each student a copy of "A True Friend" on pages 127-129 and a pen or pencil, or display a copy using an overhead projector.
• Students complete the Bible study.

A true friend is:
1. caring and available.
2. encouraging.

- - - - - - - - - - - Fold - - - - - - - - - - -

3. willing to sacrifice.
4. patient.
5. a good listener.

At first glance, which of these qualities are your greatest strengths in a friendship?

In which areas do you need improvement?

1. Caring and Available
Read these Scriptures and explain in the space provided how each relates to being a friend who deeply cares and is willing to be available to a friend in need.

Proverbs 17:17

Romans 12:15

Galatians 6:2

Which of your friends could use an extra dose of caring this week? What can you do to show you care?

2. Encouraging
The special friendship of David and Jonathan is one of the most inspiring stories in the Old Testament. How does 1 Samuel 20:17 relate to the area of encouragement in their special friendship?

In 1 Samuel 20:42, how is the Lord involved in their relationship?

Would your friends call you an encouraging person?

List three specific ways in which you can be more of an encouragement to your friends:
a.
b.
c.

3. Willing to Sacrifice
Read John 15:12,13.
What is your reaction to this Scripture?
a. Wow!
b. I'm glad Christ did that for me.
c. Impossible or at least improbable!
d. Now that's a heavy commitment.
e. Other

TEAM EFFORT

A PRICELESS GIFT

There are very few things in life as important or as wonderful as true friendship. A good friend is a treasure beyond almost anything else in life. Friendship is a priceless gift from God.

Take a moment to reflect on your friendship.

List three people you consider to be true friends. Why?

1. ....

....

2. ....

....

3. ....

....

List the names of three to five people with whom you would like to become better friends.

1. ....

....

2. ....

....

3. ....

....

4. ....

....

5. ....

....

TEAM EFFORT

FRIENDSHIP SURVEY SHEET[1]

1. How many friends do you have?

2. Do you have friends of both sexes?

3. Do you have friends who are five years younger than you?

4. Do you have friends who are five years older than you?

5. What's the craziest thing you've done with friends?

6. Who would consider you one of their friends?

7. List three qualities you have that make you a good friend.

8. What qualities does your best friend have?

9. Are your parents your friends? Why or why not?

10. Do you have more or fewer friends than you had one year ago?

11. Are you a good friend? Why?

Note

1. Adapted from Arlo Reichter, *The Group Retreat Book* (Loveland, CO: Group Publishing, 1983), p. 155. Used by permission.

IN THE WORD

A TRUE FRIEND

A true friend is:
1. caring and available.
2. encouraging.
3. willing to sacrifice.
4. patient.
5. a good listener.

At first glance, which of these qualities are your greatest strengths in a friendship?

....

....

In which areas do you need improvement?

....

....

1. **Caring and Available**

   Read these Scriptures and explain in the space provided how each relates to being a friend who deeply cares and is willing to be available to a friend in need.

   Romans 12:15

   ....

   Proverbs 17:17

   ....

   Galatians 6:2

   ....

   ....

   Which of your friends could use an extra dose of caring this week? What can you do to show you care?

   ....

   ....

2. **Encouraging**

   The special friendship of David and Jonathan is one of the most inspiring stories in the Old Testament. How does 1 Samuel 20:17 relate to the area of encouragement in their special friendship?

   ....

   ....

IN THE WORD

In 1 Samuel 20:42, how is the Lord involved in their relationship?

....

Would your friends call you an encouraging person?

....

List three specific ways in which you can be more of an encouragement to your friends:

a. ....

b. ....

c. ....

3. **Willing to Sacrifice**

Read John 15:12,13.

What is your reaction to this Scripture?

a. Wow!

b. I'm glad Christ did that for me.

c. Impossible of at least improbable!

d. Now that's a heavy commitment.

e. Other ....

What are little everyday sacrifices that we can do to deepen a friendship?

....

....

How do you think this Scripture relates to Jesus Christ being your friend?

....

Is this quality a strength or a weakness in your life? If it's a weakness, how can you become a better listener? If it is already a strength, congratulations! You, no doubt, are a positive influence in somebody's life!

....

....

....

....

....

4. **Patient**

"Love is patient" (1 Corinthians 13:4).

Why do you suppose patience is included as a quality of a true friend?

....

Think of a friend with whom you can be more patient. Write a few goals for developing a more patient attitude with him or her.

....

SO WHAT?

Now that you have investigated the true qualities of a friend, what practical changes can you make in your friendships?

....

....

....

....

5. **A Good Listener**

It has been said that listening is the language of love. Who listens to you?

....

How has his or her listening influenced your life in a positive way?

....

THINGS TO THINK ABOUT

1. Why do you think God gives us friends?

....

....

....

....

....

....

2. True friendship is costly. What do you think it takes to develop a deeper friendship?

....

....

....

....

....

....

3. Read Ecclesiastes 4:8-12. How do these verses relate to friendship?

....

....

....

....

....

PARENT PAGE

FOR THE PARENT

Who were your best friends when you were a teen?

....

....

Who would you consider your best friend now?

....

....

How did/do your friends influence your life?

....

....

What's a memorable experience you had with some friends?

....

....

For the Student

Which of your friends had a positive influence in your life?

....

....

What kinds of peer pressure do a lot of your friends experience?

....

....

Name a situation where you had to sacrifice to keep a struggling friendship going.

....

....

Discuss a situation where your parent was a friend to you.

Let's take a look at a few principles about friendship and strengthening a friendship. Check the principles you think are most important and discuss why.

.... Friends have a profound influence on your life.

.... Choose your friends wisely.

.... Be yourself. Don't try to be someone you're not.

.... Shared common experiences tend to strengthen your friendship.

.... Work at making your friendships a real priority in life.

.... Christian friends will usually encourage you to draw closer to God.

Session 8 "Friendship: A Priceless Gift"
Date ....

Unit III

SHARING YOUR FAITH

LEADER'S PEP TALK

A few years ago I stood watching the Rose Parade with my family and a million other spectators in Pasadena, California. An older man who looked like he was a few cases short of a full load shuffled up to me. I thought he was going to ask me for money because he appeared to be homeless. Instead, he told me that God told him to tell me this message, "God loves you and has a wonderful plan for your life." He then handed me a tract, and as he shuffled away he yelled back, "God bless you, sir!"

My first reaction was to laugh at him. After all, he needed a bath and who was he telling me about God's love. I had spoken the weekend before to several thousand kids about the same subject.

And then it happened. I read the little tract he gave me. Sure enough it was the simple, beautiful gospel. The printing wasn't as nice as this book, and there was no color; just a simple, black-and-white, clear message of God's love for humankind. I wondered, *Did God really tell him to speak to me? Am I really a brother of that nameless man? Was his style of sharing his faith very effective? Was he just a little crazy? Should I have been standing on the street corner of the Rose Parade preaching with a megaphone like some of the others?* You know, I still don't have all the answers, but for some reason that little bearded man with the oversized coat made an impression on my life.

I didn't take up his style of witnessing. In fact, I don't even think it's the most effective style of sharing our faith. However, the next time I used some of the material I have in this section, I was more aware that God uses all kinds of ways to reach His creation. Yet God still tends to work through us on a one-on-one basis as we learn the Great Commission and how to better communicate a lifestyle of love to a generation who hasn't responded to God. You have the opportunity to place lifelong witnessing skills into the hands of your students, and at the very least, remind many of them once again that God told us to tell them that He loves them—a whole bunch.

THE GREAT COMMISSION

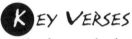EY VERSES

"Therefore go and make disciples of all nations, baptizing them in the name of the Father and of the Son and of the Holy Spirit, and teaching them to obey everything I have commanded you. And surely I am with you always, to the very end of the age." Matthew 28:19,20

BIBLICAL BASIS

Matthew 9:37; 28:16-20; Acts 1:6-11; 2 Timothy 2:2

THE BIG IDEA

Jesus commands all believers to make disciples and carry on the Christian faith.

AIMS OF THIS SESSION

During this session you will guide students to:
• Examine the words of Jesus in the Great Commission;

• Discover how the Great Commission relates to every person;
• Implement a lifestyle of following the Great Commission in their lives.

ARM UP

BLIBS—
A funny twist on the stories of two biblical characters.

TEAM EFFORT— JUNIOR HIGH/ MIDDLE SCHOOL

GOOD NEWS/ BAD NEWS—
Students experience good news and bad news.

EAM EFFORT— HIGH SCHOOL

MAKE ME AN INSTRUMENT—
A look at what it means to be used by God.

N THE WORD

FULFILLING THE COMMISSION—
A Bible study on the Great Commission.

THINGS TO THINK ABOUT (OPTIONAL)

Questions to get students thinking and talking about fulfilling the Great Commission.

ARENT PAGE

A tool to get the session into the home and allow parents and young people to discuss sharing the good news of Jesus.

LEADER'S DEVOTIONAL

"And the things you have heard me say in the presence of many witnesses entrust to reliable men who will also be qualified to teach others" (2 Timothy 2:2).

Every Wednesday morning at 5:45 A.M., a small group of five senior guys and I would crawl out of bed to meet at Bakers Square for an early morning breakfast Bible study before school. We met almost every week for a whole school year to study the Gospel of John. As we talked about the importance of following Jesus on a daily basis, three of the five guys seriously took that to heart. Now, as college students, exciting things are happening as Craig, Shane and Charles continue to fulfill the Great Commission. Craig went to Costa Rica on a month-long college mission trip and has served as a rock climbing instructor at a Christian camp. Shane has traveled to Haiti as a medical missionary. Serving junior high and high school students, Charles has faithfully learned to lead teenagers into personal relationships with Christ. (The two others? Unfortunately, one dropped out of sight and the other went to college and became a Communist. Three outta five ain't bad!)

   Paul's admonition to Timothy to find reliable men qualified to carry out the Great Commission is an important reminder of what our task is as youth workers. God wants you to be a developer of people; a disciple-maker who influences young people to bring others to Christ. The mark of an effective youth worker is not how many students are in his or her youth group, but how many students actually become disciples of Jesus Christ. The most important investment of your time and energy is discipling young people to carry out the Great Commission. That's something that they can do on their campuses, in their homes, on their sports teams and at their places of work. Young people can make a powerful difference for God in everything they do. God wants to use teenagers for His kingdom and His glory today. The Great Commission is not reserved for adults only. That's a wonderful message you get to share with the students you serve! (Written by Joey O'Connor.)

Nothing can be made more plain than that God is bent on the conquest of the world....God can employ all methods but chiefly loves to work men upon men.— Charles Wesley

THE GREAT COMMISSION

KEY VERSES

"Therefore go and make disciples of all nations, baptizing them in the name of the Father and of the Son and of the Holy Spirit, and teaching them to obey everything I have commanded you. And surely I am with you always, to the very end of the age." Matthew 28:19,20

BIBLICAL BASIS

Matthew 9:37; 28:16-20; Acts 1:6-11; 2 Timothy 2:2

THE BIG IDEA

Jesus commands all believers to make disciples and carry on the Christian faith.

WARM UP (5-10 MINUTES)

BLIBS

• Have students provide the appropriate type of word to complete the following paragraphs. Read each aloud when all the blanks are completed.

Jonah

And it came to pass that Jonah, a _____ (adjective) man, was asked by the Lord to go to _____ (place) and to tell all the people there that they should turn from their evil _____ (nouns). But Jonah, because he was _____ (adjective), refused to go, and instead decided to travel by _____ (mode of transportation) to _____ (place). However, while Jonah was asleep under the _____ (noun), the Lord caused the sea to be _____ (adjective) and decided to throw Jonah into the _____ (liquid). As Jonah swam for his life, he was swallowed by a giant _____ (animal). And Jonah found himself inside its _____ (part of body). Jonah begged the Lord for forgiveness, and

---------- Fold ----------

After the resurrection of Jesus, His disciples returned to Galilee where Jesus said He would meet them. While in Galilee He gave His disciples the Great Commission just before ascending into heaven.

Each part of the Great Commission had real significance to the disciples, and has just as much relevance to you, His disciple, today.

Let us investigate each section of the Great Commission and write out why it is significant.

"All authority in heaven and on earth has been given to me" (v. 18). On what basis could Jesus give this commission?

"Therefore go and make disciples of all nations" (v. 19). What does it mean to make disciples? How would you do that?

"Baptizing them in the name of the Father and of the Son and of the Holy Spirit" (v. 19). What significance does baptism have in this process?

"Teaching them to obey everything I have commanded you" (v. 20). What would this teaching include?

"And surely I will be with you always, to the very end of the age" (v. 20). What is the significance of Jesus' being with you?

The Great Commission and You

Who in your life needs your love, care and witness of Jesus Christ? List three people.

SO WHAT?

What can you do to begin to fulfill the Great Commission during this next week?

When Christ ascended into heaven, He entrusted the job of making disciples to people like yourself. What makes this Great Commission such an awesome task?

How do Jesus' words in Matthew 28:20 assure you of His help?

THINGS TO THINK ABOUT (OPTIONAL)

• Use the questions on page 145 after or as a part of "In the Word."

1. The Great Commission in Matthew 28:16-20 is about evangelism and disciple making. How do both of those issues fit into the Great Commission?

2. What fears do people have when it comes to telling others about Jesus Christ?

3. What challenges does the Great Commission give you personally?

PARENT PAGE

• Distribute page to parents.

was then given a second _____ (noun). He was thrown up on the _____ (noun) and with a smile across his _____ (part of body), Jonah went to do as he was told.

Noah

Many years ago, the Lord looked upon the people of the earth and saw that they were very _____ (adjective). So the Lord decided to send a great _____ (noun) that would cover the entire _____ (adjective) man, and the Lord said to Noah, "Noah, go build yourself a _____ (noun). Go out and gather up both male and female of every living _____ (noun) and put them inside the _____ (noun)." So Noah did as God instructed. And when he was _____ (adjective), the _____ (liquid) began to fall from the _____ (noun). All of the _____ (adjective) people began to cry out.

_____ (exclamation), but it did them no good. Noah sent a _____ (number) days later, the storm stopped. Noah sent a _____ (animal) out of the window to see if the ground was _____ (adjective). It flew back with a _____ (part of body) and the Lord sent a in its _____ (adjective) rainbow to let Noah know that never again would _____ (noun) He destroy the world with _____ (noun).

⊤ EAM EFFORT—JUNIOR HIGH/ MIDDLE SCHOOL (15-20 MINUTES)

GOOD NEWS/BAD NEWS

• Divide students into groups of three or four.
• Have student complete the following statements five different ways so that they are funny and five different ways so that they are serious: The good news is...; the bad news is...
• Students share responses.
• Ask the following questions:
How does it feel to receive good news?
How does it feel to receive bad news?
Read Matthew 28:16-20. What elements of good news are in the Great Commission?

⊤ EAM EFFORT—HIGH SCHOOL (15-20 MINUTES)

MAKE ME AN INSTRUMENT

• Divide students into groups of three or four.
• Give each student a copy of "Make Me an Instrument" on page 141 and a pen or pencil, or display a copy using an overhead projector.
• Students complete their pages.

- Fold -

"He said to his disciples, 'The harvest is plentiful but the workers are few'" (Matthew 9:37). Francis of Assisi was a wealthy, highborn man who lived hundreds of years ago. He felt that his life was incomplete, and even though he had more than enough wealth, he was a very unhappy man. One day, while he was out riding, he met a leper. The leper was loathsome and repulsive in the ugliness of his disease. Something moved Francis to dismount and fling his arms around this person. In the arms of Francis, the leper's face changed into the face of Christ. Francis was never the same again.

Francis of Assisi spent the rest of his life serving his Lord Jesus Christ. He wrote these famous words as a prayer to God from the heart of a man who had a deep desire to be an instrument of God's will on this earth:

Lord, make me an instrument of Your peace.
Where there is hatred, let me sow love;
Where there is injury, pardon;
Where there is doubt, faith;
Where there is despair, hope;
Where there is darkness, light;
And where there is sadness, joy.

What does Jesus mean in Matthew 9:37?

Can you think of any biblical characters with a similar story to Frances of Assisi's?

Can you think of any modern-day people with a similar story?

What makes this prayer of Francis of Assisi so important to all who want to follow Jesus?

Read Matthew 28:16-20. How does Francis of Assisi's prayer fit into the Great Commission?

Ι N THE WORD (25-30 MINUTES)

FULFILLING THE COMMISSION

• Divide students into groups of three or four.
• Give each student a copy of "Fulfilling the Commission" on page 143 and a pen or pencil, or display a copy using an overhead projector.
• Students complete the Bible study.

"Then the eleven disciples went to Galilee, to the mountain where Jesus had told them to go. When they saw him, they worshiped him; but some doubted. Then Jesus came to them and said, 'All authority in heaven and on earth has been given to me. Therefore go and make disciples of all nations, baptizing them in the name of the Father and of the Son and of the Holy Spirit, and teaching them to obey everything I have commanded you. And surely I am with you always, to the very end of the age'" (Matthew 28:16-20).

TEAM EFFORT

MAKE ME AN INSTRUMENT

"He said to his disciples, 'The harvest is plentiful but the workers are few'" (Matthew 9:37).

Francis of Assisi was a wealthy, highborn man who lived hundreds of years ago. He felt that his life was incomplete, and even though he had more than enough wealth, he was a very unhappy man. One day, while he was out riding, he met a leper. The leper was loathsome and repulsive in the ugliness of his disease. Something moved Francis to dismount and fling his arms around this person. In the arms of Francis the leper's face changed into the face of Christ. Francis was never the same again.

Francis of Assisi spent the rest of his life serving his Lord Jesus Christ. He wrote these famous words as a prayer to God from the heart of a man who had a deep desire to be an instrument of God's will on this earth:

> Lord, make me an instrument of Your peace.
> Where there is hatred, let me sow love;
> Where there is injury, pardon;
> Where there is doubt, faith;
> Where there is despair, hope;
> Where there is darkness, light;
> And where there is sadness, joy.

What does Jesus mean in Matthew 9:37?

....

....

Can you think of any biblical characters with a similar story to Frances of Assisi's?

....

....

Can you think of any modern-day people with a similar story?

....

....

What makes this prayer of Francis of Assisi so important to all who want to follow Jesus?

....

....

Read Matthew 28:16-20. How does Francis of Assisi's prayer fit into the Great Commission?

....

....

IN THE WORD

FULFILLING THE COMMISSION

"Then the eleven disciples went to Galilee, to the mountain where Jesus had told them to go. When they saw him, they worshiped him; but some doubted. Then Jesus came to them and said, 'All authority in heaven and on earth has been given to me. Therefore go and make disciples of all nations, baptizing them in the name of the Father and of the Son and of the Holy Spirit, and teaching them to obey everything I have commanded you. And surely I am with you always, to the very end of the age'" (Matthew 28:16-20).

After the resurrection of Jesus, His disciples returned to Galilee where Jesus said He would meet them. While in Galilee He gave His disciples the Great Commission just before ascending into heaven.

Each part of the Great Commission had real significance to the disciples, and has just as much relevance to you, His disciple, today.

Let us investigate each section of the Great Commission and write out why it is significant.

"All authority in heaven and on earth has been given to me" (v. 18). On what basis could Jesus give this commission?

....

....

"Therefore go and make disciples of all nations" (v. 19). What does it mean to make disciples? How would you do that?

....

....

"Baptizing them in the name of the Father and of the Son and of the Holy Spirit" (v. 19). What significance does baptism have in this process?

....

....

"Teaching them to obey everything I have commanded you" (v. 20). What would this teaching include?

....

....

"And surely I will be with you always, to the very end of the age" (v. 20). What is the significance of Jesus' being with you?

....

The Great Commission and You

Who in your life needs your love, care and witness of Jesus Christ? List three people.

....

....

When Christ ascended into heaven, He entrusted the job of making disciples to people like yourself. What makes this Great Commission such an awesome task?

....

....

How do Jesus' words in Matthew 28:20 assure you of His help?

....

....

....

....

SO WHAT?

What can you do to begin to fulfill the Great Commission during this next week?

....

....

....

....

....

....

THINGS TO THINK ABOUT

1. The Great Commission in Matthew 28:16-20 is about evangelism and disciple making. How do both of those issues fit into the Great Commission?

....
....
....
....
....
....

2. What fears do people have when it comes to telling others about Jesus Christ?

....
....
....
....
....
....

3. What challenges does the Great Commission give you personally?

....
....
....
....
....
....

PARENT PAGE

THE GREAT COMMISSION AND THE ASCENSION

"So when they met together, they asked him, 'Lord, are you at this time going to restore the kingdom to Israel?'

"He said to them: 'It is not for you to know the times or dates the Father has set by his own authority. But you will receive power when the Holy Spirit comes on you; and you will be my witnesses in Jerusalem, and in all Judea and Samaria, and to the ends of the earth.'

"After he said this, he was taken up before their very eyes, and a cloud hid him from their sight.

"They were looking intently up into the sky as he was going, when suddenly two men dressed in white stood beside them. 'Men of Galilee,' they said, 'why do you stand here looking into the sky? This same Jesus, who has been taken from you into heaven, will come back in the same way you have seen him go into heaven.'" (Acts 1:6-11).

What is the vital importance of the disciples receiving the Holy Spirit?

....
....
....
....

How are Matthew 28:16-20 and Acts 1:8 related?

....
....
....
....

What are all Christians commanded to do?

....
....
....
....

What can we as a family do to follow the Great Commission?

....
....
....
....

Session 9 "The Great Commission"

Date..

THE POWER OF AFFIRMATION AND ENCOURAGEMENT

KEY VERSES

"And let us consider how we may spur one another on toward love and good deeds. Let us not give up meeting together, as some are in the habit of doing, but let us encourage one another —and all the more as you see the Day approaching." Hebrews 10:24,25

BIBLICAL BASIS

Matthew 19:14; John 1:42; 1 Thessalonians 5:11; 2 Thessalonians 2:16,17; Hebrews 3:13; 10:24,25

THE BIG IDEA

An important part of God's work on earth is to affirm, uplift and encourage others.

AIMS OF THIS SESSION

During this session you will guide students to:

• Examine how affirmation and encouragement is an important part of everyone's leadership ministry;

• Discover the power of affirmation through study and actual affirmation exercises;

• Implement a ministry of affirmation.

WARM UP

WHERE DO YOU RECEIVE ENCOURAGEMENT?—

Students share their experiences of encouragement.

TEAM EFFORT— JUNIOR HIGH/ MIDDLE SCHOOL

AFFIRMATION BOMBARDMENT—

Students give and receive affirmation.

TEAM EFFORT— HIGH SCHOOL

AFFIRMATION YARN—

Students build up the group by affirming each other.

IN THE WORD

BE AN ENCOURAGER—

A Bible study on the impact of affirming and encouraging others.

THINGS TO THINK ABOUT (OPTIONAL)

Questions to get students thinking and talking about a ministry of affirmation.

PARENT PAGE

A tool to get the session into the home and allow parents and young people to discuss affirming each other.

LEADER'S DEVOTIONAL

"May our Lord Jesus Christ himself and God our Father, who loved us and by his grace gave us eternal encouragement and good hope, encourage your hearts and strengthen you in every good deed and word" (2 Thessalonians 2:16,17).

When my best friend, Dana, died of cancer a few years ago, it was the most devastating loss I had ever faced. Dana had been actively involved in our youth ministry and he was loved by tons of kids. His battle with cancer and subsequent death was the most difficult struggle I ever experienced. A few weeks after his death, I received a letter in the mail from a girl in our high school named Chiara. In the letter, she encouraged me with this poem:

> There is nothing—no circumstance, no testing—that can ever touch me until first of all, it has gone past God and past Christ right through to me. If it has come that far, it has come with a great purpose, which I may not understand at the moment. But as I refuse to become panicky, as I lift up my eyes to Him and accept it as coming from the throne of God for some great purpose or blessing to my own heart, no sorrow will ever disturb me, no trial will ever disarm me, no circumstance will cause me to fret. For I shall rest in the joy of what my Lord is! That is the rest of victory!

It's incredible how God uses young people to minister to youth ministers! More than anything else that others tried to say or do for me, Chiara's poem was the most encouraging thing that helped me the most in my grief over Dana's death. It gave me a whole new perspective of God's presence in the midst of my circumstances. Her encouragement to me was a powerful affirmation I've never forgotten.

In Jesus Christ, you can offer eternal encouragement to the young people with whom you work. The power of affirmation and encouragement can and will change their lives. To say an encouraging word or affirm the qualities you see in a teenager doesn't take long, but it sure goes a long way in the life of a student dying for attention. Every student wants someone to believe in him or her. Your positive words of encouragement and affirmation can be the very things to lead young people from death to life. (Written by Joey O'Connor.)

Many a time a word of praise or thanks or appreciation or cheer has kept a man on his feet. Blessed is the man who speaks such a word.— William Barclay

THE POWER OF AFFIRMATION AND ENCOURAGEMENT

KEY VERSES

"And let us consider how we may spur one another on toward love and good deeds. Let us not give up meeting together, as some are in the habit of doing, but let us encourage one another—and all the more as you see the Day approaching." Hebrews 10:24,25

BIBLICAL BASIS

Matthew 19:14; John 1:42; 1 Thessalonians 5:11; 2 Thessalonians 2:16,17; Hebrews 3:13; 10:24,25

THE BIG IDEA

An important part of God's work on earth is to affirm, uplift and encourage others.

WARM UP (5-10 MINUTES)
WHERE DO YOU RECEIVE ENCOURAGEMENT?

• Divide students into groups of three or four.
• Have students sit in a circle while they take turns completing the following statements:
  The most encouraging person I know is...
  One of the most encouraging experiences of my life was...
  I hope I can be more encouraging to others by...

TEAM EFFORT—JUNIOR HIGH/ MIDDLE SCHOOL (15-20 MINUTES)
AFFIRMATION BOMBARDMENT

• Divide students into groups of six or seven.
• Give each student a sheet of paper and a pen or pencil.
• Students write an affirming word about each person in their groups. Then take one person at a time and have all the other students bombard him or her with a word of affirmation.

Fold

3.
4.
5.
Who can you give praise to and what will you do?

SO WHAT?
Be Available.
"Jesus said, 'Let the little children come to me, and do not hinder them, for the kingdom of heaven belongs to such as these'" (Matthew 19:14).
Why do you think Jesus was available even to younger brothers and sisters?

How can you help people by being more available?

THINGS TO THINK ABOUT (OPTIONAL)
• Use the questions on page 159 after or as a part of "In the Word."
1. Why do you think Jesus made affirmation such an important part of His ministry?

2. How can affirmation be a positive way to share your faith with another person?

3. What is it like to be around a person who never has anything good to say about others?

PARENT PAGE
• Distribute page to parents.

AFFIRMATION YARN

- Divide students into groups of six or seven.
- Give a ball of yarn, string or rope to one person. Whoever is holding the yarn affirms someone else in the group and then tosses the yarn to that person. That person affirms someone else and tosses the yarn to that person. Make sure everyone gets affirmed.

IN THE WORD (25-30 MINUTES)

BE AN ENCOURAGER

- Divide students into groups of three or four.
- Give each student a copy of "Be an Encourager" on pages 153-157 and a pen or pencil, or display a copy using an overhead projector.
- Students complete the Bible study.

1. The Word on Encouragement
The Bible challenges us to share our faith through encouragement and affirmation. Read each verse and write out how you can apply the principle of encouragement given in it.

I Thessalonians 5:11

Hebrews 3:13

Hebrews 10:24,25

a. How have you been encouraged by someone this past month?

b. Why is it sometimes so difficult to give and receive encouragement from our families?

c. List several ways God has encouraged humankind.

d. On a scale from 1 to 10 rate how often you encourage others.

1	2	3	4	5	6	7	8	9	10
Never		Seldom		Sometimes			Often		Always

2. Smile, God Loves You!
a. God affirms you. Webster's Dictionary says that to affirm means to say positively; declare firmly; assert to be true. What are a few ways God has affirmed you?

You can be an encourager! In fact you are called by God to be an encourager to whomever He places in your life.
To get a better perspective of how you can do this, answer the questions below.

b. God loves you. What are specific ways you know God loves you?

c. God believes in you. What do you think it means to have God believe in you?

d. God draws out the best in you. What positive personality trait is God helping you to develop? (Examples: patience, caring, becoming a more affirming person.)

One of the most important qualities a Christian can have is the ministry of affirmation. When we give people the gift of affirmation, we are giving them something far greater than material gifts. American psychologist William James said, "The deepest principle in human nature is the craving to be appreciated."

3. The Ministry of Affirmation
As you read about Jesus you'll see over and over again in the gospels that He had the power to draw out the best in people. Remember when He met a clumsy, big-mouthed fisherman named Simon? He looked straight into Simon's eyes and said, "So you are Simon the son of John." Simon nodded. Then Jesus said, "You will be called Cephas (which, when translated, is Peter)" (John 1:42). Jesus nicknamed him Cephas or Peter, which means "The Rock."

Peter's friends or family probably laughed at the new name Jesus gave him. Apparently he had anything but a "rock" of a personality. They would have never believed that this uneducated fisherman would someday be a leader of the Christian Church.

Jesus saw beyond Peter's problems, beyond his personality quirks and beyond his sin. Jesus turned Peter's weaknesses into strengths. He believed in Peter, and He had the power to draw out the best in Peter. Peter changed. It took years, but in the New Testament we see a man who was transformed by the power of God because Jesus affirmed him.

a. Believe in people.
You have the power to affect lives by the way you believe in people. Because God believes in you, as a Christian you can believe in others. Here's a quote about one of the world's great religious leaders: "He refused to see the bad in people. He often changed human beings by regarding them not as what they were but as though they were what they wished to be." It is very important to praise those around you. They will appreciate it and respond to praise. Be generous with your praise!
List three people who need your belief in them. In other words, who are your Simon Peters?
1.
2.
3.

b. Be liberal with praise.
"Therefore encourage one another and build each other up, just as in fact you are doing" (I Thessalonians 5:11).
Mark Twain once said, "I can live two months on one good compliment."
People respond to praise. Make a list of different ways you can give the gift of affirmation. (For example: Write a note to a friend, tell someone in your family about your love for him or her, send flowers.)
1.
2.

IN THE WORD

BE AN ENCOURAGER

1. The Word on Encouragement

The Bible challenges us to share our faith through encouragement and affirmation.

Read each verse and write out how you can apply the principle of encouragement given in it.

1 Thessalonians 5:11

....

....

Hebrews 3:13

....

....

Hebrews 10:24,25

....

....

You can be an encourager! In fact you are called by God to be an encourager to whomever He places in your life. To get a better perspective of how you can do this, answer the questions below.

a. How have you been encouraged by someone this past month?

....

....

b. Why is it sometimes so difficult to give and receive encouragement from our families?

....

....

c. List several ways God has encouraged humankind.

....

....

d. On a scale from 1 to 10 rate how often you encourage others.

1	2	3	4	5	6	7	8	9	10
Never		Seldom		Sometimes			Often		Always

IN THE WORD

2. Smile, God Loves You!

a. God affirms you. Webster's Dictionary says that to affirm means to say positively; declare firmly; assert to be true. What are a few ways God has affirmed you?

....

....

b. God loves you. What are specific ways you know God loves you?

....

....

c. God believes in you. What do you think it means to have God believe in you?

....

....

d. God draws out the best in you. What positive personality trait is God helping you to develop? (Examples: patience, caring, becoming a more affirming person.)

....

....

One of the most important qualities a Christian can have is the ministry of affirmation. When we give people the gift of affirmation, we are giving them something far greater than material gifts. American psychologist William James said, "The deepest principle in human nature is the craving to be appreciated."

3. The Ministry of Affirmation

As you read about Jesus you'll see over and over again in the gospels that He had the power to draw out the best in people. Remember when He met a clumsy, big-mouthed fisherman named Simon? He looked straight into Simon's eyes and said, "So you are Simon the son of John." Simon nodded. Then Jesus said, "You will be called Cephas (which, when translated, is Peter)" (John 1:42). Jesus nicknamed him Cephas or Peter, which means "The Rock."

Peter's friends or family probably laughed at the new name Jesus gave him. Apparently he had anything but a "rock" of a personality. They would have never believed that this uneducated fisherman would someday be a leader of the Christian church.

Jesus saw beyond Peter's problems, beyond his personality quirks and beyond his sin. Jesus turned Peter's weaknesses into strengths. He believed in Peter, and He had the power to draw out the best in Peter. Peter changed. It took years, but in the New Testament we see a man who was transformed by the power of God because Jesus affirmed him.

a. Believe in people.

You have the power to affect lives by the way you believe in people. Because God believes in you, as a Christian you can believe in others. Here's a quote about one of the world's great religious leaders: "He refused to see the bad in people. He often changed human beings by regarding them

155 © 1995 by Gospel Light. Permission to photocopy granted.

IN THE WORD

not as what they were but as though they were what they wished to be." It is very important to praise those around you. They will appreciate it and respond to praise. Be generous with your praise!

List three people who need your belief in them. In other words, who are your Simon Peters?

1. ....

2. ....

3. ....

b. **Be liberal with praise.**

"Therefore encourage one another and build each other up, just as in fact you are doing" (1 Thessalonians 5:11).

Mark Twain once said, "I can live two months on one good compliment."

People respond to praise. Make a list of different ways you can give the gift of affirmation. (For example: Write a note to a friend, tell someone in your family about your love for him or her, send flowers.)

1. ....

2. ....

3. ....

4. ....

5. ....

Who can you give praise to and what will you do?

....

....

SO WHAT?

Be Available.

"Jesus said, 'Let the little children come to me, and do not hinder them, for the kingdom of heaven belongs to such as these'" (Matthew 19:14).

Why do you think Jesus was available even to younger brothers and sisters?

....

....

....

How can you help people by being more available?

....

....

....

Things to Think About

1. Why do you think Jesus made affirmation such an important part of his ministry?

....

....

....

....

....

2. How can affirmation be a positive way to share your faith with another person?

....

....

....

....

....

3. What is it like to be around a person who never has anything good to say about others?

....

....

....

....

....

....

....

....

PARENT PAGE

"And let us consider how we may spur one another on toward love and good deeds. Let us not give up meeting together, as some are in the habit of doing, but let us encourage one another—and all the more as you see the Day approaching" (Hebrews 10:24,25).

How can we as a family encourage one another?

....

....

....

....

What kind of encouragement could you use from your family at this time?

....

....

....

....

The Family Affirmation List

Each family member can use this list to communicate encouragement. You can also make up more of your own areas of affirmation.

1. What I especially appreciate about you is...
2. One of my favorite memories of you and I is...
3. You made my day when...
4. If I could give you a gift of affirmation it would be...

Action step: Positive time together is one of the greatest sources of affirmation and encouragement. Take a moment to plan a special outing together in the next month.

Session 10 "The Power of Affirmation and
Encouragement" Date ....

SHARING THE GOOD NEWS

KEY VERSE

"But God demonstrates his own love for us in this: While we were still sinners, Christ died for us." Romans 5:8

BIBLICAL BASIS

Genesis 3; Exodus 20:1-17; Psalm 51:4,5; Isaiah 53:5; 59:1,2; 64:6; Habakkuk 1:13; Matthew 5:13-16; Mark 7:21-23; John 1:12; 3:16; 5:24; 10:10; 15:22; Romans 3:9,20,23; 5:1,2,8-11; 6:17,23; 7:9,15-20; 8:31-34; 10:9; Galatians 5:19-21; Ephesians 1:7; 2:1-3,8,9; Philippians 2:14,15; Colossians 1:20-22; 1 Timothy 2:5; Titus 3:3,5; James 4:17; 1 Peter 3:18; 1 John 1:5,6; 3:4; 5:11-13; Revelation 3:20

THE BIG IDEA

God's plan of salvation is woven through-out the Scriptures and can be offered as good news to a fallen world.

AIMS OF THIS SESSION

During this session you will guide students to:
• Examine the good news of the gospel;
• Discover God's plan of salvation and how they can be prepared to share that good news with others;
• Implement how to share the good news.

WARM UP

MOTHER I'M SICK, MOTHER I'M DYING—

A skit of varying emotion.

TEAM EFFORT— JUNIOR HIGH/ MIDDLE SCHOOL

GIVING TO OTHERS—

A story of the ultimate giving to others.

TEAM EFFORT— HIGH SCHOOL

THE GREAT FISH CONTROVERSY—

A story on the importance of reaching others with the good news.

IN THE WORD

THE PLAN OF SALVATION—

A Bible study on God's plan to redeem His people.

THINGS TO THINK ABOUT (OPTIONAL)

Questions to get students thinking and talking about the good news of Jesus.

PARENT PAGE

A tool to get the session into the home and allow parents and young people to discuss being salt and light to their world.

LEADER'S DEVOTIONAL

"But he was pierced for our transgressions, he was crushed for our iniquities; the punishment that brought us peace was upon him, and by his wounds we are healed" (Isaiah 53:5).

As a freshman, Brandon came to our youth ministry almost on a fluke. Someone had given him a flyer at school about a free burger bash, so he and a friend showed up to our mid-week outreach event. After coming to the burger bash, Brandon began to regularly show up each week. Off and on for the next year, Brandon came and learned what being a Christian was all about. Then, one night he finally gave his life to Christ.

About a year later, Brandon signed up for one of our snow-ski trips to Utah. One day, while Brandon and I were riding up the ski lift, I asked him what convinced him to make a commitment to Christ. Brandon said he always remembered a simple story I told about how a Father sacrificially allowed His Son to die so that others could live. If God was willing to do that for him, Brandon figured, then it wouldn't be much for him to give his life to God.

Simple stories change lives. The Gospel is a simple story filled with good news that continues to change a fallen world. Sharing God's good news is one of the greatest privileges we have as Christians. When young people grasp the significance and simplicity of the gospel, powerful things happen. That's why your influence in their lives is so critical. That's why being a youth worker is one of the highest callings to which you could ever respond. When you share the good news with a young person, you are having a tremendous impact on all their future decisions—where they go to school, how they will treat their friends, whom they choose to date and marry and how they raise their children. Sharing the good news of Jesus Christ sparks a chain reaction of God's love through untold thousands of lives. (Written by Joey O'Connor.)

"Evangelism is just one beggar telling another beggar where to find the bread."—D.T. Niles

SHARING THE GOOD NEWS

KEY VERSE

"But God demonstrates his own love for us in this: While we were still sinners, Christ died for us." Romans 5:8

BIBLICAL BASIS

Genesis 3; Exodus 20:1-17; Psalm 51:4,5; 59:1,2; 64:6; Habakkuk 1:13; Matthew 5:13-16; Mark 7:21-23; John 1:12; 3:16; 5:24; 10:10; 15:22; Romans 3:9,20,23; 5:1,2,8-11; 6:17,23; 7:9,15-20; 8:31-34; 10:9; Galatians 5:19-21; Ephesians 1:7; 2:1-3,8,9; Philippians 2:14,15; Colossians 1:20-22; 1 Timothy 2:5; Titus 3:3,5; James 4:17; 1 Peter 3:18; 1 John 1:5,6; 3:4; 5:11-13; Revelation 3:20

THE BIG IDEA

God's plan of salvation is woven throughout the Scriptures and can be offered as good news to a fallen world.

WARM UP (5-10 MINUTES)
MOTHER I'M SICK, MOTHER I'M DYING

- Before class, assign skit roles.
- Give each performer a copy of "Mother I'm Sick, Mother I'm Dying" on page 167.
- Students perform skit.

TEAM EFFORT—JUNIOR HIGH/ MIDDLE SCHOOL (15-20 MINUTES)
GIVING TO OTHERS

- Divide students into groups of three or four.
- Give each student a copy of "Giving to Others" on page 169 and a pen or pencil, or display a copy using an overhead projector.
- Students complete their pages.

--- Fold ---

The Response and Result

1. Our response
   John 1:12; Romans 10:9; Revelations 3:20
2. The result
   John 5:24; Romans 5:1,2; 9-11
3. The promise and assurance
   1 John 5:11-13

Answer these questions:

1. According to these Scriptures, what must we do to be saved?

2. What makes these Scriptures such good news?

Now summarize "the response and results" to share with the rest of the group.

So What?
How can we use this material to benefit our lives? How can we use this material to benefit the kingdom of God?

THINGS TO THINK ABOUT (OPTIONAL)

- Use the questions on page 177 after or as a part of "In the Word."

1. The gospel means "good news." What makes the gospel of Christ such good news?

2. If the gospel is such good news, why doesn't everyone accept it?

3. How does 1 Timothy 2:5 fit into the plan of salvation?

PARENT PAGE

- Distribute page to parents.

A little boy was told by his doctor that he could actually save his sister's life by giving her some blood. The six-year-old girl was near death, a victim of a disease from which the boy had made a marvelous recovery two years earlier. Her only chance for restoration was a blood transfusion from someone who had previously conquered the illness. Since the two children had the same rare blood type, the boy was the ideal donor.

"Johnny, would you like to give your blood for Mary?" the doctor asked. The boy hesitated. His lower lip started to tremble. Then he smiled and said, "Sure, Doc. I'll give my blood for my sister."

Soon the two children were wheeled into the operating room—Mary, pale and thin; Johnny, robust and the picture of health. Neither spoke, but when their eyes met, Johnny grinned.

As his blood siphoned into Mary's veins, one could almost see new life come into her tired body. The ordeal was almost over when Johnny's brave little voice broke the silence. "Say, Doc, when do I die?"

It was only then that the doctor realized what the moment of hesitation, the trembling of the lip, had meant earlier. Little Johnny actually thought that in giving his blood to his sister he was giving up his life! And in that brief moment, he had made his great decision!

1. What were Johnny's conditions for giving to Mary?

2. What are your conditions for giving to another?

⊤EAM EFFORT—HIGH SCHOOL (15-20 MINUTES)

THE GREAT FISH CONTROVERSY

• Divide students into groups of three or four.
• Give each student a copy of "The Great Fish Controversy" on page 171 and a pen or pencil, or display a copy using an overhead projector.
• Students complete their pages.
• Read story aloud.

1. What's the main point of this story?

2. What can we do to keep this story from being the story of our lives?

IN THE WORD (25-30 MINUTES)

THE PLAN OF SALVATION

• Divide students into three groups: The Problem, The Solution, and The Response and Result.
• Give each student a copy of "The Plan of Salvation" on pages 173-175 and a pen or pencil, or display a copy using an overhead projector.
• Students complete their pages.
• Have students share their responses.

---- Fold ----

The Problem
1. Sin—what is it?
   Psalm 51:4,5; James 4:17; 1 John 3:4
2. How did sin originate?
   Genesis 3
3. How do we know about sin?
   Exodus 20:1-17; Romans 3:20, 7:9,15-20
4. Who sins?
   John 15:22; Romans 3:9,23
5. The result of sin
   a. Stray from God
      Isaiah 59:1-2; Habakkuk 1:13; Ephesians 2:1-3; 1 John 1:5,6
   b. We become slaves to sin
      Mark 7:21-23; Romans 6:17; 8:31-34; Galatians 5:19-21; Titus 3:3
   c. Spiritual death
      Romans 6:23
6. We cannot "remedy" this condition
   Isaiah 64:6; Romans 3:20; Ephesians 2:8,9; Titus 3:5

Answer these questions:

1. Why does sin pose such a problem for God?

2. Why did sin separate God and humankind?

Now summarize "the problem" to share with the rest of your group.

The Solution
1. God's plan
   John 3:16; 10:10
2. God's remedy: The Cross
   Romans 5:8; Ephesians 1:7; Colossians 1:20-22; 1 Peter 3:18

Answer these questions:

1. What makes the Cross central to our salvation?

2. Could there have been another remedy to reconcile God and humankind?

Now summarize "the solution" to share with the rest of your group.

MOTHER I'M SICK, MOTHER I'M DYING[1]

Characters:

Doctor   Son (or Daughter)

Mother   Director

First try: Make it as dry as possible, like it is being read for the first time. No expression at all. When Director stops it, he claims this is an emotional scene and the actors should sound emotional.

Second try: Do it with wild emotion; it is the saddest thing you have ever seen. When Director stops he says that maybe the actors have overdone it a little—make it a bit lighter.

Third try: It is now the funniest thing that could ever have happened; laugh until it hurts. Director tells the actors, after this try, to mix it up a little and add a little variety.

Fourth try: Son—redo first try, as deadpan as possible. Mother—redo second try in complete hysteria. Doctor—redo third try, again laugh until it hurts. Director stops practice and says, "I think I am dying."

Mother: (enter)

Son: (enter) Mother, I feel sick.

Mother: Son, you look sick.

Son: Mother, I think I will die.

Mother: Oh, Son, you must not do that. I will call the doctor. (Pick up phone) Doctor, Doctor, come quickly, my son is dying.

Doctor: (enter immediately as Mother finishes)

Mother: Doctor, where have you been?

Doctor: I had an emergency appendectomy after you called.

Son: (after slight pause) I feel sick.

Mother: You look sick.

Son: I am sick. (slight pause) I think I will die.

Mother: You must not die.

Doctor: You are dying.

Son: I am dying.

Director stops the practice.

Note

1. Source unknown.

TEAM EFFORT

GIVING TO OTHERS

A little boy was told by his doctor that he could actually save his sister's life by giving her some blood. The six-year-old girl was near death, a victim of a disease from which the boy had made a marvelous recovery two years earlier. Her only chance for restoration was a blood transfusion from someone who had previously conquered the illness. Since the two children had the same rare blood type, the boy was the ideal donor.

"Johnny, would you like to give your blood for Mary?" the doctor asked. The boy hesitated. His lower lip started to tremble. Then he smiled and said, "Sure, Doc. I'll give my blood for my sister."

Soon the two children were wheeled into the operating room—Mary, pale and thin; Johnny, robust and the picture of health. Neither spoke, but when their eyes met, Johnny grinned.

As his blood siphoned into Mary's veins, one could almost see new life come into her tired body. The ordeal was almost over when Johnny's brave little voice broke the silence. "Say, Doc, when do I die?"

It was only then that the doctor realized what the moment of hesitation, the trembling of the lip, had meant earlier. Little Johnny actually thought that in giving his blood to his sister he was giving up his life! And in that brief moment, he had made his great decision!

1. What were Johnny's conditions for giving to Mary?

2. What are your conditions for giving to another?

TEAM EFFORT

THE GREAT FISH CONTROVERSY[1]

For months, the Fisher's Society had been wracked with dissension. They had built a new meeting hall which they called their Aquarium and had even called a world renowned Fisherman's Manual scholar to lecture them on the art of fishing. But still no fish were caught.

Several times each week they would gather in their ornate Aquarium Hall, recite portions of the Fisherman's Manual and then listen to their scholar exposit the intricacies and mysteries of the manual. The meeting would usually end with the scholar dramatically casting his net into the large tank in the center of the hall and the members rushing excitedly to its edges to see if any fish would bite. None ever did, of course, since there were no fish in the tank. Which brings up the reason for the controversy.

The temperature of the tank was carefully regulated to be just right for ocean perch. Indeed, oceanography experts had been consulted to make the environment of the tank nearly indistinguishable from the ocean. But still no fish. Some blamed it on poor attendance at the Society's meetings. Others were convinced that specialization was the answer. Perhaps several smaller tanks geared especially for different fish age group would work. There was even division over which was more important: casting or providing optimum tank conditions. Eventually a solution was reached.

A few members of the Society were commissioned to become professional fishermen and were sent to live a few blocks away on the edge of the sea and do nothing but catch fish. It was a lonely existence because most other members of the Society were terrified of the ocean. So the professionals would send back pictures of themselves holding some of their catches and letters describing the joys and tribulations of real live fishing. And periodically they would return to Aquarium Hall to show slides. After such meetings, people of the Society would return to their homes thankful that their Hall had not been built in vain.

1. What's the main point of this story?

....

....

....

2. What can we do to keep this story from being the story of our lives?

....

....

....

....

Note

1. This story was originally given as a sermon by Ben Patterson at Irvine Presbyterian Church in Irvine, California.

IN THE WORD

THE PLAN OF SALVATION
The Problem
1. Sin—what is it?

   Psalm 51:4,5; James 4:17; 1 John 3:4
2. How did sin originate?

   Genesis 3
3. How do we know about sin?

   Exodus 20:1-17; Romans 3:20; 7:9,15-20
4. Who sins?

   John 15:22 ; Romans 3:9,23
5. The result of sin

   a. Stray from God

      Isaiah 59:1,2; Habakkuk 1:13; Ephesians 2:1-3; 1 John 1:5,6

   b. We become slaves to sin

      Mark 7:21-23; Romans 6:17; 8:31-34; Galatians 5:19-21; Titus 3:3

   c. Spiritual death

      Romans 6:23
6. We cannot "remedy" this condition

   Isaiah 64:6; Romans 3:20; Ephesians 2:8,9; Titus 3:5;

Answer these questions:

1. Why does sin pose such a problem for God?

....

....

2. Why did sin separate God and humankind?

....

....

Now summarize "the problem" to share with the rest of your group.

....

....

The Solution
1. God's plan

   John 3:16; 10:10
2. God's remedy: The Cross

   Romans 5:8; Ephesians 1:7; Colossians 1:20-22; 1 Peter 3:18

 **IN THE WORD**

Answer these questions:

1. What makes the Cross central to our salvation?

....

....

2. Could there have been another remedy to reconcile God and humankind?

....

....

Now summarize "the solution" to share with the rest of your group.

....

....

The Response and Result

1. Our response
   John 1:12; Romans 10:9; Revelations 3:20
2. The result
   John 5:24; Romans 5:1,2; 9-11
3. The promise and assurance
   1 John 5:11-13

Answer these questions:

1. According to these Scriptures, what must we do to be saved?

....

....

2. What makes these Scriptures such good news?

....

....

Now summarize "the response and results" to share with the rest of the group.

....

....

SO WHAT?

How can we use this material to benefit our lives? How can we use this material to benefit the kingdom of God?

....

....

....

....

THINGS TO THINK ABOUT

1. The gospel means "good news." What makes the gospel of Christ such good news?

....

....

....

....

....

....

2. If the gospel is such good news, why doesn't everyone accept it?

....

....

....

....

....

....

3. How does 1 Timothy 2:5 fit into the plan of salvation?

....

....

....

....

....

....

....

....

PARENT PAGE

SALT AND LIGHT: ADDING FLAVOR AND SIGHT TO THE WORLD

"You are the salt of the earth. But if the salt loses its saltiness, how can it be made salty again? It is no longer good for anything, except to be thrown out and trampled by men. You are the light of the world. A city on a hill cannot be hidden. Neither do people light a lamp and put it under a bowl. Instead they put it on its stand, and it gives light to everyone in the house. In the same way, let your light shine before men, that they may see your good deeds and praise your Father in heaven" (Matthew 5:13-16).

In this passage, what two images does Jesus use to describe His disciples?

....

....

....

Before refrigeration, salt was used to keep meat from rotting. With this in mind, what do you think Jesus meant when He said, "You are the salt of the earth" (v. 13)?

....

....

....

What might cause Christians to lose their saltiness?

....

....

....

How can a Christian be a "light of the world" (v. 14)?

....

....

....

Read Philippians 2:14,15. What does Paul advise Christians to do in order to be light in the world?

....

....

....

Why do you think "light" is such a common reference to Christ and faith in Him?

....

....

....

PARENT PAGE

The Christian Taste Test

Circle the appropriate answer:

If I am salt, my relationship with Christ is:

blah   tasteless   mild   seasoned   spicy   very tasty

Complete the following sentence:

To add more "salt" to my Christian diet, I need to...

....

Turned on for Jesus

Circle the response that best describes you.

When it comes to shining for Christ, I...

     a.   shine brightly.

     b.   flicker now and then.

     c.   feel dark and cold.

     d.   need a new spark.

     e.   burn hotter every day.

     f.   shed the light of God's glory.

     g.   need a few other candles for help.

If Jesus came to you today and said, "I need you. You are My only light to your family, friends, and school or work. Will you shine for Me?" What would you say and do?

....

....

Who Are You Influencing?

Billy Graham, the well known evangelist, once said, "The evangelistic harvest is always urgent. The destiny of men and nations is always being decided. Every generation is strategic. God will hold us responsible as to how well we fulfill our responsibilities to this age and take advantage of our responsibilities."

How do you feel when you hear that you are strategic for reaching your generation for God?

....

....

....

What can you as a family do to fulfill your God-given responsibilities?

....

....

....

Session 11 "Sharing the Good News"

Date ....

WITNESSING SKILLS

KEY VERSES

"We proclaim him, admonishing and teaching everyone with all wisdom, so that we may present everyone perfect in Christ. To this end I labor, struggling with all his energy, which so powerfully works in me." Colossians 1:28,29

BIBLICAL BASIS

Acts 26:1-23; Colossians 1:28,29; 4:5,6

THE BIG IDEA

As Christ has redeemed our lives we can share that good news with others.

AIMS OF THIS SESSION

During this session you will guide students to:

• Examine various ways of sharing their faith stories;

• Discover a method of sharing their faith and witnessing for Jesus Christ;

• Implement a lifestyle of sharing their faith in a positive way.

WARM UP

SHARING OUR STORY—

Students develop stories of their own.

TEAM EFFORT— JUNIOR HIGH/ MIDDLE SCHOOL

THE WITNESS—

A role-play of one way to share the faith.

TEAM EFFORT— HIGH SCHOOL

THE 60-SECOND INFOMMERCIAL FOR CHRIST—

Students "sell" their stories of Jesus.

IN THE WORD

SHARING YOUR TESTIMONY—

A Bible study on developing a testimony of faith.

THINGS TO THINK ABOUT (OPTIONAL)

Questions to get students thinking and talking about their testimonies of Christ's work in their lives.

PARENT PAGE

A tool to get the session into the home and allow parents and young people to discuss their faith experiences.

LEADER'S DEVOTIONAL

"Be wise in the way you act toward outsiders; make the most of every opportunity. Let your conversation be always full of grace, seasoned with salt, so that you may know how to answer everyone" (Colossians 4:5,6).

One of the most effective ways I've discovered to communicate the gospel to teenagers is to have a young person speak instead of me. Many times in youth ministry, youth workers believe that they have to make a gospel presentation "just right" before they speak to young people. While it's important to present the message of Jesus Christ clearly, I've found that it doesn't have to be presented perfectly. Let me give you an example.

John was involved in our youth ministry and had a tremendous conversion to Christ. Previously, John was heavily involved in the party scene and was very popular on campus. When John made a commitment to Christ, he was then in a position to be a positive influence in other students' lives. From time to time, I asked John to either give his testimony or to speak at our midweek program. John wasn't a polished speaker. He didn't always say things as well as they could have been said, but the most important thing was that John was authentic. John simply shared how Jesus transformed his life and how Jesus could do the same for anyone else. When John spoke, other students listened. John was one of their own.

Your youth ministry is the best place for students to learn how to share their faith. And some of the best communicators of the gospel in your youth ministry may not be adults, but teenagers! If we're really serious about young people making a difference in this world for Jesus Christ, then we must give them the opportunity to communicate how God has changed their lives. As you spend time with teenagers, you are sharing the life of Jesus Christ with them. Watch what will happen in your ministry when your students begin doing the same thing with their family and friends! (Written by Joey O'Connor.)

"The life of a preacher speaks louder than his words."—Oswald Chambers

WITNESSING SKILLS

KEY VERSES

"We proclaim him, admonishing and teaching everyone with all wisdom, so that we may present everyone perfect in Christ. To this end I labor, struggling with all his energy, which so powerfully works in me." Colossians 1:28,29

BIBLICAL BASIS

Acts 26:1-23; Colossians 1:28,29; 4:5,6

THE BIG IDEA

As Christ has redeemed our lives we can share that good news with others.

WARM UP (5-10 MINUTES)

SHARING OUR STORY

• Divide students into groups of three or four.
• Have each group compose one paragraph of a story using one or more of the following words: alligator, wicked princess, hero, castle, early morning, horse, lost map and happily ever after.
Then have each group compose one paragraph about God using one or more of the following words: love, Jesus, cross, resurrection, eternal life, freedom, joy and response.

TEAM EFFORT—JUNIOR HIGH/ MIDDLE SCHOOL (15-20 MINUTES)

THE WITNESS

• Assign the skit roles.
• Give each performer a copy of "The Witness" on pages 187-189. If possible, do this before the session so performers have an opportunity to rehearse.
• Students perform skit.

- Ask students the following questions:
  What do you see as the key twist in this drama?
  What are better ways to share our faith?

TEAM EFFORT—HIGH SCHOOL (15-20 MINUTES)

THE 60-SECOND INFOMMERCIAL FOR CHRIST

- Divide students into groups of three or four.
- Have each group prepare a 60-second infommercial for Christ. They can use take-offs from recent TV commercials or create their own.
- Videotape each group, and show the results to the whole group.
- As a whole group, discuss the pros and cons of presenting the love of Christ in a 60-second and infommercial.

IN THE WORD (25-30 MINUTES)

SHARING YOUR TESTIMONY

- Divide students into groups of three or four.
- Give each student a copy of "Sharing Your Testimony" on page 191 and a pen or pencil, or display a copy using an overhead projector.
- Students complete the Bible study.

Paul's Testimony
Read Acts 26:1-23.
After reading Paul's testimony, take a few minutes to fill in the blanks as if you were a modern-day Paul.
Before I met Jesus Christ:

How I met Jesus Christ:

How Christ has changed my life:

So What?

Now that you have read Paul's testimony, here's a chance for you to write out your own testimony. Your testimony might not be as dramatic as Paul's, but you can use the same formula as found in Acts 26:1-23 to write your own account of meeting Christ.
Before I met Christ:

How I met Christ:

How Christ has changed and is changing my life:

Share your testimony with your group.

THINGS TO THINK ABOUT (OPTIONAL)

- Use the questions on page 193 after or as a part of "In the Word."
1. What makes it difficult to share our faith stories with others?
2. How have you seen witnessing done in a negative way? In a positive way?
3. What makes the personalization of a testimony so important?

PARENT PAGE

- Distribute page to parents.

TEAM EFFORT

THE WITNESS[1]

The scene is a typical student union. Joe is seated at a table studying in preparation for an upcoming test. Nick, a super-straight-looking student, approaches and sits right next to Joe ignoring all the empty seats around him.

Nick: Hi...How ya doin'?...Do you live around here?

Joe: (Eyes still on books.) Yea.

Nick: Where?...Where do you live?

Joe: (Still reading.) In the dorms.

Nick: Really?...I thought about living there once...What's it like? (Pause. Joe doesn't answer.) Do you study here all the time?

Joe: (Concentration finally broken, gives Nick a hard look.) Yes, I study here a lot because over in the dorms too many people bother me, and I can't concentrate!

Nick: Yea, it must be really hard to study with people bothering you all the time.

Joe: Yes, it is!

Nick: (Begins talking faster, acts rather nervous and unsure.) Are you saved?

Joe: What?

Nick: Are you saved? You see, I belong to the Go With God Student Christian Club, and we are sort of taking a survey to see who is going to hell. But you don't have to go to hell. (Nick pulls out a booklet called "God Wants You!") Right here in this little book is a chance for you to have eternal life. Here on page one it says "You are hiding from God in the wretchedness of your ugly sins. You must repent."

Joe: (He is dumbfounded and speechless until this point.) Wait a minute...

Nick: Oh, please save your questions until I've read you the whole thing.

Joe: In case it's not obvious, I'm trying to study.

Nick: There are only three more pages. Now this verse from the Bible...

Joe: (Louder.) I am not interested in your weird religious ideas!

Nick: (Pause.) What's your name?

Joe: My name isn't important. Will you please go away so I can study.

Nick: If you don't listen to me, your name, whatever it is, won't be written in the book of life and...

Joe: (Very mad, he explodes.) Look! I am trying to study, or are you too ignorant to see that? What is it with you Jesus freaks anyway? Do you work on a commission basis? One more star in your halo for every soul saved! Well, I'm not interested, so flake off!

Nick: (Pause, dead serious.) He said we would be persecuted.

Joe: (Resigned.) I don't believe this! (Slams book shut, rips booklet in half, throws it in Nick's face and storms off mumbling something about crazy fanatics. Nick rises and stands in center stage.)

Mr. Applegate: (From the darkness behind Nick.) That was very good Nick.

Nick: (His whole composure changed to a strong determined person.) That wasn't just "very good."

Mr. Applegate: (He comes into the light with Nick. He wears a dark business suit, and there is something ominous about him.) How do you mean?

TEAM EFFORT

Nick: That was the best you've ever seen. I know it, you know it, and Number One knows it.

Mr. Applegate: That's why I have come to talk to you. Number One has a new assignment for you.

Nick: It's about time.

Mr. Applegate: There is a new church and coffee house which has just opened on the north side. The man who runs it has a very intimate relationship with the Enemy. He is very dangerous and could change our whole standing there without fast action. Number One seems to think that you are creative enough to come up with some good moves. We'll start you as a heroin pusher, but if you can't work with that let us know and other arrangements can be made. Can you handle it?

Nick: I can.

Mr. Applegate: Good. Let me warn you Nick, we don't usually let demons of your standing take a job like this. If you fail...well you know what will happen.

Nick: I know.

Mr. Applegate: Very well. You'll start right away...

Note

1. *Ideas Number 21-24* (El Cajon, CA: Youth Specialties, 1984), pp. 109-111. Used by permission.

IN THE WORD

SHARING YOUR TESTIMONY[1]

Paul's Testimony

Read Acts 26:1-23.

After reading Paul's testimony, take a few minutes to fill in the blanks as if you were a modern-day Paul.

Before I met Jesus Christ:

....

....

How I met Jesus Christ:

....

....

How Christ has changed my life:

....

....

SO WHAT?

Now that you have read Paul's testimony, here's a chance for you to write out your own testimony. Your testimony might not be as dramatic as Paul's, but you can use the same formula as found in Acts 26:1-23 to write your own account of meeting Christ.

Before I met Christ:

....

....

How I met Christ:

....

....

How Christ has changed and is changing my life:

....

....

Share your testimony with your group.

Note

1. Adapted from Barry St. Clair, *Giving Your Faith Away* (Wheaton, IL: Victor Books, 1991). Used by permission.

THINGS TO **T**HINK **A**BOUT

1. What makes it difficult to share our faith stories with others?

....

....

....

....

....

....

2. How have you seen witnessing done in a negative way? In a positive way?

....

....

....

....

....

....

....

3. What makes the personalization of a testimony so important?

....

....

....

....

....

....

PARENT PAGE

THE FAITH ROAD MAP

"We proclaim him, admonishing and teaching everyone with all wisdom, so that we may present everyone perfect in Christ. To this end I labor, struggling with all his energy, which so powerfully works in me" (Colossians 1:28,29).

As a family, share key moments in your spiritual life that have brought you to where you are today. You can use conversion experiences, difficult periods, special times with God or other significant moments. Start with your oldest recollection of a key Christian experience and move toward the present time.

....
....
....
....
....
....
....
....
....
....
....
....
....
....
....
....
....
....
....
....

Session 12 "Witnessing Skills"

Date..................................

Add a New Member to Your Youth Staff.

Jim Burns is president of the
National Institute of Youth Ministry.

 Meet Jim Burns. He won't play guitar and he doesn't do windows, but he will take care of your programming needs. That's because his new curriculum, **YouthBuilders Group Bible Studies** is a comprehensive program designed to take your group through their high school years. (If you have jr. high kids in your group, **YouthBuilders** works for them too.)

For less than $6 a month you'll get Jim Burns' special recipe of high-involvement, discussion-oriented, Bible-centered studies. It's the next generation of Bible curriculum for youth—and with Jim on your staff, you'll be free to spend more time one-on-one with the kids in your group.

Volume One of the YouthBuilders curriculum series is:
The Word on Sex, Drugs & Rock 'n' Roll
ISBN 08307.16424
**Look for these issues in other
volumes of Youthbuilders:**
- Prayer and the Devotional Life
- The Basics of Christianity
- Being a Leader, Serving Others and Sharing Your Faith
- Servanthood, Commitment and Discipleship
- Crisis Issues and Peer Counseling

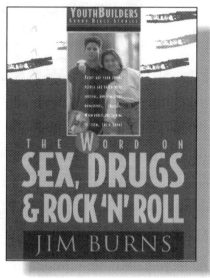

Here are some of YouthBuilders hottest features

- Reproducible pages–
  one book fits your whole group
- Wide appeal–
  big groups, small groups–even adjusts to fit jr. high/high school groups
- Hits home–
  special section to involve parents with every session of the study
- Interactive Bible discovery–
  geared to help young people find answers themselves
- Cheat sheets–
  a Bible *Tuck-In*™ with all the session information on a single page
- Flexible format–
  perfect for Sunday mornings, midweek youth meetings, or camps and retreats
- Three studies in one–
  each study has three, four-session modules examining critical life choices.

A Push-Button Course for Junior High.

Jr. High Builders are all-in-one programs that help kids put their faith in action. Each book in the series includes 13 Bible studies, dozens of games and activities as well as clip art to illustrate your handouts—all you have to do is warm up the copier!

Jr. High Builders titles include:
- Christian Basics (ISBN 08307.16963)
- Christian Relationships (ISBN 08307.16491)
- Symbols of Christ (ISBN 08307.15126)
- Power of God (ISBN08307.17048)
- Faith in Action (ISBN 08307.17056)
- Life-Styles of the Not-so-Famous from the Bible
  (ISBN 08307.17099)
and many others - 12 in all!

Gospel Light

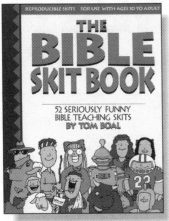

More Books and Resources from Jim Burns.

These and other great books and resources are available from your local Christian bookstore
or from Jim Burns' National Institute of Youth Ministry (NIYM)
P.O. Box 4374, San Clemente, CA 92674. Phone 714-498-4418.

 **Drug-Proof Your Kids**
Stephen Arterburn & Jim Burns
Solid biblical principles are combined with effective prevention and intervention techniques to equip Christian parents to prepare or work through the growing crisis of alchoholism that prevails in our youth.

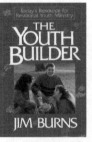 **The Youth Builder**
Today's Resource for Relational Youth Ministry
Jim Burns
This Gold Medallion Award winner provides you with proven methods, specific recommendations and hands-on examples of handling and understanding the problems and challenges of youth ministry.

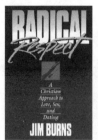 **Radical Respect**
A Christian Approach to Love, Sex, and Dating
Jim Burns
Without compromising biblical convictions, Jim Burns balances real-life situations with God's orginal design for dating in the '90s. Written directly to youths, Burns addresses common questions about love, sex and dating.

 **When Love Is Not Enough**
Stephen Arterburn & Jim Burns
Arterburn and Burns offer understanding and practical tools to deal with crisis situations as well as guidelines to help any family prevent problems before they develop.

 **Putting God First**
Jim Burns
A workbook for youth to make God their first priority and to understand God's blessings for those who follow Him.

 **Radically Committed**
Jim Burns
Packed with straight talk, challenging questions and practical exercises, **Radically Committed** will take the reader through accepting Christ as their savior and making a radical difference for Christ in their walk.

 High School Ministry
Mike Yaconelli & Jim Burns
Especially written for high-school youth workers, learn about the youth and the influence of their culture and discover the tremendous impact you can have on your kids.

 **Spirit Wings**
A Devotional for Youth
Jim Burns
In the language of today's teens, these 84 short devotionals will encourage youth to build a stronger and more intimate relationship with God.

 Surviving Adolescence
Jim Burns
In **Surviving Adolescence**, Jim Burns involves parents and youth workers to help kids make wise choices in making friends, peer pressure, dating, sex, drugs and other important decisions.

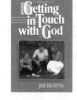 **Getting in Touch with God**
Jim Burns
Develop a consistent and disciplined time with God in the midst of hectic schedules as Jim Burns shares with you inspiring devotional readings to deepen your love for God.